Conversations with Maryse Condé

Conversations with
Maryse Condé

Françoise Pfaff

University of Nebraska Press, Lincoln and London

An earlier version of this work
was published as *Entretiens
avec Maryse Condé* (Paris:
Editions Karthala, 1993).

© 1996 by the University
of Nebraska Press

Manufactured in the United
States of America
⊛ The paper in this book meets
the minimum requirements
of American National
Standard for Information
Sciences – Permanence of
Paper for Printed Library
Materials, ANSI Z39.48-1984.
Library of Congress
Cataloging-in-Publication Data
Condé, Maryse. [Entretiens
avec Maryse Condé. English]
Conversations with Maryse
Condé / Françoise Pfaff.
p. cm. Includes biblio-
graphical references and
index. ISBN 0-8032-3713-8
(cl : alk. paper). –
ISBN 0-8032-8743-7
(pa : alk. paper)
1. Condé, Maryse – Interviews.
2. Authors, Guadeloupe –
20th century – Interviews.
I. Pfaff, Françoise. II. Title.
PQ3949.2.C65Z46613 1997
843 – dc20 96-11057 CIP

This work is dedicated to my Alsatian and Guadeloupean ancestors

Contents

Illustrations

Following page 74

Preface

Acclaimed in France, Africa, and the Caribbean, Maryse Condé is a novelist, playwright, essayist, and author of short stories and children's books. With her provocative characters, arresting themes, beautifully crafted language, and innovative narrative techniques, she is widely recognized as one of the most original talents to appear on the French and Francophone literary scene in recent years. Her contributions to contemporary literature won her the coveted French awards Le Grand Prix Littéraire de la Femme (1986) and Le Prix de l'Académie Française (1988).

Many of Maryse Condé's novels have been translated into English and other languages and are now appreciated by a broad international readership. U.S. literary critics praise her writings, and her books are taught at a number of American universities. Master's theses and doctoral dissertations have been dedicated to her works. Condé received a Guggenheim fellowship and was the first woman honored as a Puterbaugh Fellow by the University of Oklahoma.

Born in 1937, the last child in a middle-class family from the French Caribbean island of Guadeloupe, Maryse Condé spent a controlled and uneventful childhood, which made her seek solace, comfort, and adventure in the books in her father's library. Soon, the vagaries of her imagination compensated for the monotony of her life, which was perhaps the early starting point for her own literary interests. When she was eight, she wrote a one-act play dedicated to her mother.

At age sixteen, Condé left Guadeloupe for Paris, where she completed high school and attained university degrees in French, classics, and English. During that period, she exchanged ideas with French, Caribbean, and African students and developed an awareness of Third World issues, such as anticolonialism and decolonization. In 1959 she married a stage actor from Guinea, Mamadou Condé.

As has often been the case for members of the Black Diaspora exiled oceans away from the land of their ancestors, Maryse Condé decided to go to Africa. She first taught for a year in the Ivory Coast, then joined her husband in Guinea, where they lived from 1960 to 1964. There, she was fascinated by the beauty of the people and inspired by her discovery of Mandingo culture and the legacies of former empires.

At first an admirer of Guinean President Sékou Touré, Maryse Condé was quick to perceive the dictatorial and oppressive aspects of his regime. This political disenchantment, added to marital difficulties, caused her to depart from Guinea with her four children. She then taught French for two years in Ghana, where she met such prominent African political figures as Kwame Nkrumah, Agostinho Neto, and Amilcar Cabral. Caught in the turmoil of the overthrow of Nkrumah, Ghana's head of state, Condé was arrested, imprisoned, and deported. She moved to London, where she worked for two years as a radio producer for the BBC foreign desk.

The next stage of what Condé terms her "nomadic" life took her to Senegal, where she met Richard Philcox, an Englishman who later became her husband and translator. In 1970 Condé returned to Paris to pursue university studies. While there, she worked as an editor for Présence Africaine publishers and enjoyed numerous encounters with Caribbean and African writers. In 1975 she received a doctorate in Caribbean literature from the Sorbonne, which allowed her to teach at the University of Paris.

Already the author of essays in literary criticism and of two theater plays, Condé began her career as a novelist with the publication of *Heremakhonon* (1976). Soon her expertise on West Indian authors and her involvement in creative writing made her a sought-after scholar. She was invited to teach at Occidental College, the University of California, the University of Virginia, the University of Maryland, and Harvard University. After a brief sojourn in Guadeloupe in the mid-1980s, Maryse Condé and Richard Philcox established residence in the United States. Condé is currently professor of French and Francophone literatures at Columbia University. She divides her time between the United States and her native Guadeloupe.

Maryse Condé's reputation and fame are linked to her talents as a novelist whose works contain a spectrum of fictional characters – Caribbean, African, and African-American – which mirror countless experiences in the wake of slavery, colonialism, and diasporic migrations. *Heremakhonon* and *A Season in Rihata* vividly recount, in an intimate mode, the existential self-searching of French Caribbean women in unnamed African countries. Also set in Africa, yet branching out to Brazil, England, and Jamaica, Condé's best-selling *Segu* and *The Children of Segu* are spectacular multigenerational sagas depicting the grandeur and decline of a Malian family in the midst of turbulent conflicts between Muslims and animists.

I, Tituba, Black Witch of Salem reflects the writer's return to the Americas, as it unravels, amidst contemporary overtones and postmodern irony, the captivating fictionalized story of a seventeenth-century slave from Barbados "forgotten" by history. *Tree of Life* recounts the gripping odyssey of a family that moves from Guadeloupe to Panama, the United States, and Europe over most of the twentieth century. *Crossing the Mangrove* vibrantly creates a microcosmic portraiture of Guadeloupean society by using the voices of multiple characters at the wake for a mysterious stranger.

Condé's two most recent novels, published in the early 1990s, have not yet appeared in English. Both works illustrate past and present contexts in the Americas and Africa. *Les derniers rois mages* (literally, The last Magi) spins a fascinating tale about the imaginary offspring engendered on the French Caribbean island of Martinique by Behanzin, the exiled king of Dahomey. *La colonie du nouveau monde* (Colony of the New World) narrates the elaborately tragic fate met by a religious sect in Colombia.

Maryse Condé, an accomplished literary creator with considerable insight into social and political issues, intermingles fiction, history, and contemporary realities. She is a prolific, provocative, and often ironic writer who excels in exploring the conditions of exile, alienation, broken family bonds, and racial matters. She develops richly textured plots with story lines that constantly shift in space and time and avoid, at all costs, folkloric and stereotypical renditions of Africa and the Caribbean islands.

Maryse Condé adds a vigorous voice to those of other internationally known West Indian authors such as Aimé Césaire, Derek Walcott, George Lamming, V. S. Naipaul, Edouard Glissant, Simone Schwarz-Bart, Myriam Warner-Vieyra, and Patrick Chamoiseau. Maryse Condé is rightly hailed as a major writer of our age.

Acknowledgments

I wish to extend my thanks and appreciation to Maryse Condé for her availability and friendly support throughout the preparation of this book. Heartfelt thanks to James H. Kennedy and María Roof for their careful reading of the text, without which this translation would be overly peppered with Gallic spices. Thanks also to Claire Méhat for help in preparing the final chapter; to Laverne Brandon Page, Cynthia Burton, and Valerie Wheat for their bibliographical expertise; and to Bertha Railsback Roof for her skillful proofreading.

I am grateful to Howard University and the National Endowment for the Humanities for their financial support.

Introduction

The genesis of *Conversations with Maryse Condé* dates back to 1981, when I first met the Guadeloupean author at Howard University in Washington DC. She, who would briskly climb the ladder of literary fame with novels such as *Segu, I, Tituba, Black Witch of Salem*, and *Tree of Life*, had come to the nation's capital to lecture on French West Indian women writers. I was impressed by the knowledge, dynamism, and humor of the lecturer, whom I would subsequently come to know better.

This book is the fruit of informal conversations that took place over a number of years in France and the Americas, stopping points on a journey through space and time reflecting Maryse Condé's own itinerary. The transcribed text has been only lightly edited in order to preserve the candor and integrity of these verbal exchanges, while also avoiding the pitfalls of self-censorship. Consequently, certain ruptures in tone and discontinuities in theme may occur, as is natural in conversations. This is the price for maintaining the authenticity, spontaneity, and familiarity of the initial words.

Conversations with Maryse Condé does not in the least aspire to be an exhaustive exegesis of the author's writings. It is a dialogue about her biographical sojourns (West Indies, Europe, Africa, United States) and literary paths, her personality and thoughts, and the connections between her life and her works. In her encounters with historical figures and opinions on politics and culture, Maryse Condé is a witness to her time.

This book is meant for a diverse readership. Those who know Maryse Condé will recall the often ironic verve of this talented novelist, playwright, and essayist. Others will discover a writer whose humanism transcends borders. The interviews provide an innovative framework for viewing works by Maryse Condé, situating them within the context of West Indian, French, and world literatures. The extensive bibliography reflects the international impact of Maryse Condé's writings.

A first version of this book was published in French as *Entretiens avec Maryse Condé* by Editions Karthala (Paris, 1993). This edition in English has been augmented by a new chapter on Maryse Condé's recent works, based on a 1994 interview. The bibliography has been expanded and updated. The University of Colorado selected this text for a Eugene M. Kayden National Translation Meritorious Achievement Award in 1995.

The published translations listed in the bibliography have been used for direct quotations. Otherwise, translations are my own.

Conversations with Maryse Condé

A Plural Life

I

FRANÇOISE PFAFF Maryse, I would like for us to explore your life to see how it has influenced your literary works. In *Tree of Life* (*La vie scélé-rate*) Albert, the forefather, dreams of his childhood while he is in the arms of a French prostitute, but his granddaughter Thécla rebels against her childhood. Seen in a positive or negative light, childhood appears to be a very important theme in your works. Would you talk about your childhood in Guadeloupe?

MARYSE CONDÉ Actually, I believe that my childhood was not at all inter-esting. I was born on February 11, 1937, the last of eight children, and so I was rather spoiled. Nothing unusual happened. I remember that we used to go to school, then take a walk around the Place de la Victoire. On Sundays we would go to church.

FP Were you a good student at school?

MC I was always at the head of my class, but I also had the reputation of being a very arrogant child. I remember never receiving the top award for overall excellence. Back then, they had impressive awards cere-monies and kids would go up on stage wearing crowns and such. My name would be called ten or fifteen times as I swept up lots of first prizes. But I never got the top award because I was considered obnox-ious, sarcastic, and ill-tempered. I was always being punished and kept in on Thursdays and Saturdays. I had a reputation as a child nobody liked very much.

FP Were you a rebel?

MC No, I just didn't like to obey the teachers.

FP Was this the sin of pride at such an early age?

MC Maybe, probably.

FP All this took place in Pointe-à-Pitre?

MC Yes. We would spend our vacations at Petit-Bourg. Otherwise, nothing much happened. My mother was in the civil service, and we used to go to Paris every five years, which was also rather boring. We would stay in apartment buildings where other West Indians lived, so even in Paris we were in a Caribbean environment. Life changed a little when I was left at a boarding school in Paris. Being so far from my parents had a very sad side to it, but I think that's when I discovered lots of things like the cinema, art, museums, and exhibitions. Those times were parentheses when I was fairly free to do whatever I wanted, and that really appealed to me and had a certain charm. Except for this, I believe that a Guadeloupean childhood, at least in the social milieu to which I belonged, was totally conventional and quite monotonous. I don't have particularly fond memories of it.

FP How would you describe your social milieu?

MC My mother was a schoolteacher, one of the first Black women of her generation to teach. My father and some friends had founded a small savings and loan company that was prosperous at the time, though it eventually went bankrupt. We were the children of prominent people, so there were certain things we had to do. First of all, we couldn't mix with just anybody. We were not allowed to speak to the other Negroes living on the same street, of course. We could not socialize with mulattoes, because they were illegitimate children of Whites. Obviously, we were not to mingle with Whites either. They were the enemy. We lived in isolation and displayed contempt for everything that was different from us, a kind of arrogance that was one of my parents' main traits, especially of my mother. We were also totally bored, because being by ourselves all the time was not very enriching. If I had belonged to a more working-class milieu, maybe I would have had one of those childhoods you read about in novels, filled with songs, stories, and fragrances. But frankly, this is not what I knew.

FP Since you lived in Pointe-à-Pitre in an urban environment, did you know much about nature?

MC My parents had a "change of air" place, as we used to call it, next to a stream in Sarcelles, Petit-Bourg. My father liked the country a lot, so we would go there as soon as school let out. He would immediately put on old, gray, banana-stained clothes and grab a machete. He pretended to be a peasant and was very happy. But for us kids, Sarcelles was a lost corner of the world, and once again we were by ourselves. We had bikes but couldn't let the country kids ride them. We would go swimming in a very pretty stream named La Rose. Or we would go to the beach, always by ourselves. Occasionally, our cousins would visit. Since they were poor, we laughed at them and made fun of their bad table manners. That was it. Nothing else happened.

FP Is the *Mandingo marabout* in your novel *Heremakhonon* (*Hérémakhonon*) somewhat like your father, whom you've talked about – very rigid and eager to do honor to the race?

MC My father was not rigid. I think he was a typical West Indian man of his time. He wasn't interested in his children. I really don't know what interested him.

FP Women?

MC No. He seemed to be pretty much in love with his wife. Maybe he was interested just in her and was deeply involved in his work and his own things. With his small bank, he had the impression of doing something important for the race.

FP A Guadeloupean business created by a Black man was indeed important.

MC My father was not alone. He worked with friends, some of whom were mulattoes. He was rather proud of being part of this group of people. He would make loans to government workers, which kept him very busy. My father had a sort of double life: one in the city and one in the country, where he fulfilled his dream of being close to nature. His father was already an urban Black. Maybe he had a farming grandfather who had impressed him a great deal.

FP Was your father's father also a businessman?

MC No. I am not really sure what he did. I only know that he was born in the city.

FP When your father's business failed, wasn't it a disaster for him?

MC The bank collapsed after his death. At the beginning, it was called Caisse Coopérative des Prêts, then it became La Banque Antillaise, which couldn't resist the onslaught of big banks like the BNP, Crédit Lyonnais, and others. The bank was resold and became, I believe, the BSC. My father didn't live to see all of this. Right up to his death, he was a man who worked in an enterprise that he thought was important.

FP Did your father have a political ideology linked to the economic independence he wanted to achieve through his banking firm?

MC Not at all. He was simply pleased with what he considered his success. He bought a lot of houses and the Sarcelles property, which was quite pretty. He had a car. At that time, not many Black men had all that, so he was happy with his success. My mother had more political awareness than he did. She had a keener understanding of race and may have been more ambitious than my father. She had photos of African-Americans all around her bedroom.

FP Who were they? Booker T. Washington? Frederick Douglass?

MC No, I don't think so. They were pictures you see in *Ebony*, middle-class African-American families, the ones called the "First Families." She compared herself to those people.

FP Did she speak English? Did she have any contacts with the Black intelligentsia in the Caribbean British islands or in the United States?

MC Not at all.

FP In so many of your literary works, there are conflicts between daughters and mothers that reappear almost obsessively. What kind of relationship did you have with your mother?

MC People are mistaken if they seek literal transcriptions of real-life relationships in novels. If I have put so much emphasis on mother-daughter conflicts in my works, it is precisely because I have never had any with my mother and few with my daughters. I am quite fascinated by what I hear from female friends who have daughters. In my case, I was the last child in the family and my mother died when I was about twenty. I didn't have time to get into conflicts with her.

FP Isn't there a connection between you and *Heremakhonon*'s female protagonist, whose father says of her: "She's insane! So headstrong! All those brains and nothing but foolish ideas" [Philcox translation, 3].

MC There is some connection. My father said that once because he wanted me to come back to Guadeloupe. He was getting older and had been widowed. As for me, because of my memories of a boring childhood, I truly did not want to return and preferred to go live in Africa. One of my sisters had married a man from Guinea and was living there. I joined her, and my father couldn't understand why two of his daughters were living in Africa. I recall that he was quite hurt and sad when I made that decision. He would say: "I wonder what Maryse is looking for in Africa. . . ."

FP In your works you allude to color-based social hierarchies in the West Indies. Did your family define itself in any particular way in terms of color?

MC My parents wanted to socialize only with Black people. They were racists in their own way, believing, as I said, that mulattoes were bastards and Whites, the enemy. Blacks who were not "successful" were considered failures. Consequently, my parents would associate only with Blacks, and even then, with just a small group of Blacks.

FP Blacks who had "succeeded"?

MC Those who were like them. They and their friends formed a terribly closed world. I don't even know what is left of that world. When I returned to Guadeloupe, I didn't try to locate my parents' friends, and I believe that this sort of people, this arrogant, closed Black caste, no longer exists.

FP Your parents socialized with well-known people. You once mentioned to me that Governor Félix Eboué was one of their friends.

MC I think he was the godfather of one of my brothers, or the person in charge of him while my parents were in France. I didn't know him personally.

FP Let's return to your childhood for a moment. Was there really nothing striking about it? Not even a teacher who had an impact on you?

MC I considered all teachers terribly boring. I always thought the courses and classes at school were dreadfully boring. The only professor I found a little interesting, amusing, was the gym teacher. I tended to be lazy, but we got along well. One day she made a mistake in French. I don't remember what she said, but it was incorrect. I corrected her in front of the whole class, and this caused a split between us. Nevertheless, I liked her a lot. That is the only recollection I have.

FP Wasn't there a literature teacher who gave birth to your interest in writing?

MC Yes, in Paris when I studied at the Lycée Fénelon. In the *hypokhâgne* [upper-level class], I met truly remarkable teachers who inspired their students to think.

FP How did you spend your adolescence?

MC I spent the first part of my adolescence in Guadeloupe and the rest in Paris, where I felt very free. I didn't have the barriers I had in Guadeloupe, where we had to be home by 6:00 p.m. and couldn't go dancing because my father was against it. He didn't want men to hold his daughters in their arms. In Paris there was a certain amount of freedom. You could breathe there, and I really loved being in Paris.

FP It was a new independence for you. Didn't the separation from your mother have a strong impact on you?

MC No. I would go back to Guadeloupe for vacations, and I don't remember suffering because of the separation. But I must add that I had brothers and sisters in Paris.

FP You didn't feel abandoned?

MC No. I had a sister and a brother studying in Paris, and one of my sisters there was my godmother. I spent every weekend with my family.

FP I understand that your sisters were much older than you and were like mothers. . . .

MC Yes. The closest child to me was my brother Guy, who was eleven years older. My sisters were fourteen or fifteen years older and acted like little mothers. They used to spoil me a lot.

FP There wasn't any rivalry among the children?

MC Not that I can recall.

FP Was it an ideal situation, then?

MC My brothers and sisters were too old to feel they had to compete with me. My sisters probably had rivalries among themselves, but I was not aware of it because I was so much younger.

FP Were you sixteen when you went to Paris?

MC Yes, when I went there to stay, though I had visited several times before. I recall having gone to nursery school in the 7th arrondissement in Paris when I was five or six years old. Of course, I was the only little Black girl at the school. I remember that on one occasion, one of my sisters put a red ribbon in my hair, and the teacher took pictures.

FP When you went to live in Paris, did you feel socially alienated or at ease right away?

MC Frankly, when I left Guadeloupe at age sixteen, I joyfully drew a line through it. I told myself I wouldn't return very soon. Nothing could pull me back there except my parents, whom I would want to visit out of affection. Unfortunately, my mother died after I went to stay in Paris. She was my only significant link to Guadeloupe. Once she was gone, Guadeloupe didn't matter to me very much.

FP What you say is puzzling because the descriptions of Paris in your books are quite negative. Paris is always very gray, the city of loneliness.

MC I don't quite see in which book I described Paris. I may have vaguely mentioned it in *Heremakhonon*, in the encounter in the streets of Paris between the heroine and a street sweeper. But the place where they meet is not that important.

FP In *Tree of Life*, when Albert arrives in Paris, he finds it to be a cold city.

MC Yes, but Albert is the one speaking. Personally, I loved Paris when I was a student because it had an essential element for me, freedom. Later on, I met a girl whose father was a Marxist historian teaching at the Sorbonne, and we became very good friends. Actually, she is the first one who mentioned things I had never thought about, like anticolonialism and decolonization. Because of her, and thanks to her, I got interested in politics. We joined the Communist Youth together, and I began to look at the world differently. That's when I realized I had to break away from the comfortable life I was leading. I tried to seek out African students who were quite aware politically.

FP What year was this?

MC It must have been in the mid-1950s. I remember going with my friend to a meeting of the Federation of Black African Students (called FEAN), where I saw and heard Sékou Touré. That was before 1958, when Guinea was not yet independent. Modibo Keita also came to address the group. I think from that point on, I became more or less politicized.

FP That's when you developed political consciousness?

MC "Political consciousness" may be too strong a term. Let's say that I acquired some sort of political sense. I suddenly realized that the Black world was not limited to Guadeloupe, where, based on my childhood, nothing much was happening. I thought that Africa would perhaps generate new experiences for me. It's not talked about much, but the end of the 1950s was a very interesting time in Paris. Jean Genêt's *The Blacks* was being staged by director Roger Blin. I went to see this play, which was the highlight of the theater season, and that's where I met my first husband, an actor playing the part of Archibald. Through him I started to get more involved with Africans. From then on, I thought it was stupid to bore myself any longer preparing entrance exams for specialized colleges. I stopped studying and finally was dismissed from school.

FP During the time you were still a serious student, what were you like in class? Did you talk back to the teachers?

MC I had discovered that they were somewhat racist. They considered me a strange animal or an exception. In the final analysis such behavior was paternalistic, and as I grew more politically aware, I also became more lucid as far as they were concerned. After being dismissed from the school, I went to study at the university.

FP What was your area of study?

MC I studied French, Latin, and Greek, as well as English. I received a B.A. in English and advanced certificates, as they were called, in Classical Letters. Then I married Mamadou Condé and left for Africa.

FP Wasn't it paradoxical for a politically conscious person, who had become interested in the contribution of Blacks to Western civilization, to specialize in Greek and Roman literature?

MC No, because I was doing two things at the same time. There was also my B.A. in English. In fact my studies allowed me to gain a good knowledge of French literature, which appealed to me, and to learn about English literature and culture, which also began to interest me. I remember starting a program for the D.E.S. [Diplôme d'Etudes Supérieures], an advanced university degree, based on a study of the voyages of discovery to Africa undertaken by early European explorers such as Mungo Park, René Caillié, and others.

FP You met Condé, married him, and left for Africa. This was a rather sudden decision. Going to Africa didn't cause you any problems?

MC No, I very happily left for Africa. There was no conflict at all.

FP What was your reaction when you first arrived there? Was it love at first sight? Were you terribly shocked?

MC Neither, because I did not go directly to Guinea with my husband. First I went to the Ivory Coast, where I had a teaching appointment at the junior high school in Bingerville, which at the time seemed to be out in the boondocks. Nowadays people can get there in the wink of an eye.

FP Chronologically speaking, are we now in Africa's postindependence era?

MC No, we are exactly in 1960.

FP Were you sent to the Ivory Coast by the French Ministry of Cooperation?

MC Yes. I had gotten married in August 1959 but my husband didn't go with me, I don't remember exactly why. But in any event, he was not with me, so I was by myself. Probably we were already not getting along.

Since I was pregnant and very young, the small West Indian community in the Ivory Coast took me under its wing. We had a West Indian–style christening for my first daughter, Sylvie, who was born on April 3, 1960, at the Abidjan Hospital. I lived in Bingerville for a year without any interest in Africa. I didn't see it. I didn't pay attention to it.

FP Did you tend to look down on Ivory Coast people?

MC No, they were of no interest to me. Apart from the West Indians, who did I know in Bingerville? A few African colleagues who wouldn't speak to me.

FP In your classes you had African children to whom you were teaching French. What grades did you teach?

MC I taught eighth and ninth grades. The most important thing that year, 1960, was that my husband asked me to join him in Guinea to show Sylvie to his family, which was the normal thing to do. We met there for summer vacation. Sylvie was a few months old. Two years earlier, Guinea had obtained independence under the leadership of Sékou Touré. Guinea seemed so extraordinary to me that I fell in love with it at first sight. I had never seen anything like it.

FP Was it more extraordinary than the Ivory Coast?

MC As I said, for me, the Ivory Coast had no reality. It had trees and was green, thick with woods. Forests, that's all. In Guinea, I was primarily struck by the beauty of the people. There were descendants and memories of the Empire of Mali, which I discovered. There was a whole Mandingo world I didn't know. There was Niane's book *Sundiata, an Epic of Old Mali*, which had just been published. There was the extraordinary discovery of a culture and civilization that excited me, as Mali did later on. Besides, we were in the midst of a revolutionary era. It was unique! I experienced a privileged moment during those years and fell in love with the country.

FP And you were in love with a man.

MC No longer, but the country reenergized our marriage, so I stayed in Guinea and worked in Conakry.

FP Were you still working as a teacher sent by the French Ministry of Cooperation?

MC No, because there were no ministry-sponsored people in Guinea. Sékou Touré's Guinea had just said "no" to de Gaulle. The Guinean government gave local contracts to foreigners. I spent my first year in Guinea in a kind of euphoria.

FP Was it an ephemeral happiness?

MC Yes. I quickly met people who were Marxist militants and who gave me books to read. Thanks to them, I evolved from political daydreaming to a true political consciousness and then to a rather deep Marxist faith. I realized that what was left in Guinea was the exploitation of the people, peasants, workers, and students. When the strikes, the great teachers' plot of 1962, took place, I was in an excellent position to observe what was happening.

FP Did you actively participate in the strikes?

MC No, I didn't.

FP What role did you play, then?

MC None. I had friends who were militants and some of them were arrested.

FP Were all these people teachers?

MC Almost all of them. Some were arrested the day after we shared a dinner, during which they discussed the presentations they would make the following day at a teachers conference.

FP What were their demands?

MC They thought that people talked about socialism but that Guinea was not socialist at all. There was no freedom of speech or freedom of expression. There was a growing gap between rich and poor. Djibril Tamsir Niane had written a rather humorous poem denouncing those who had lined their pockets after the country's independence while the majority of the population became more impoverished. He was arrested. Following his arrest, students called the strikes I mentioned in *Heremakhonon*. Niane was principal of the Donka high school and was adored by the students. A student whom I liked very much was arrested and disappeared. We later learned that he was tortured. So right away, I had something other than my first idyllic view of Guinea. These events taught me that state power could prevent people from being happy, from living, from doing what they wanted. Years later, this experience generated the title of my book *Heremakhonon*, meaning "Wait for happiness."

FP In your eyes, Sékou Touré had become a dictator and a torturer?

MC Yes, that was how I saw him because people were arrested and some were deported. The repression was really very brutal. I saw soldiers drive a truck into the compound of the junior high school where I taught and beat up students.

FP You also describe this kind of military abuse in *A Season in Rihata* (*Une saison à Rihata*). Was all of this inspired by the events in Guinea?

MC Yes, indeed.

FP Did you have contacts with government people?

MC Not at all. I was not important enough. My husband was related to a government minister, Keita Fodéba, but as a relative without great financial means, he was not highly esteemed and was never invited to anything. I, his foreign wife, was given even less consideration.

FP Didn't you get personally harassed in the course of these events?

MC I was nothing but a privileged witness. Let me stress again that I was a foreigner married to a Guinean who had no political opinions. Consequently, there was no reason to harass me. I am the one who decided to leave Guinea because I could not see why I was staying there. I left in 1964. My marriage had gone down the drain anyway.

FP What was your husband's occupation in Guinea?

MC In Paris he had been an actor. When he returned to Guinea, he became director of the National Ballet, but he couldn't do his job because people would constantly poke sticks in his wheels. This is what happens in our countries. He had studied in France and married a "White woman," which is what I was called. He was suspect for these reasons. He couldn't get anything done. Everything he proposed flopped. It was quite an infernal life!

FP Was Sylvie still your only child?

MC No, Aïcha was born a year after Sylvie, in 1961. Then Leïla was born in 1963. Condé had a son by his first wife whom we brought to live with us, along with my son Denis. There were five children in all, and I was very busy taking care of all these kids.

FP It was indeed rather generous on your part to take care of your husband's child by another woman.

MC Later I regretted it, because he turned out to be quite a difficult child. He was one of the reasons I left Guinea.

FP Was he older than your own children?

MC No, not much, two or three years older than Denis. I had insisted that my widowed mother-in-law come to live with us. I didn't know that between Condé's mother and his son from a first union, my life would become totally impossible.

FP What was the relationship like between you and your mother-in-law?

MC Atrocious. She hardly spoke French, only Malinke. When she spoke to me, it was to say things to me that I found unthinkable. I realize now that we could not get along because of too many cultural differences. At the time, I limited myself to putting up with her hostility. But personal difficulties were piling up on top of political problems, and that's why I left. I absolutely had to leave if I wanted to go on living.

FP Aside from your mother-in-law's animosity and your close relationships with militant teachers, how were you generally received in Guinea?

MC When I arrived, people accepted me at first without any problem, because it seemed that I was going to become part of the Malinke community. Problems began when people realized that, although I was a Black woman married to a Guinean man, I was different from them. I came from "elsewhere." I didn't speak Malinke, was not Muslim, and didn't know how to cook Guinean food. There were a great many customs I didn't know or understand. And so a chasm grew. I can't say it was a rejection exactly, but certainly a very sharp sense of distance. No one was prepared to accept my difference. Had I been French or German or Swedish, that is to say, a White woman, people would have expected different behavior from me and, one way or another, would have made the best of it. In my case they did not.

FP Did you make an effort to integrate linguistically by learning to speak Malinke?

MC People have to help you make such an effort. Since I was enduring a sort of cultural terrorism, I reacted to it by refusing to integrate. I am not someone who is very flexible by nature, and I told myself that people were not going to change me overnight. I was different, and people had to accept my difference instead of ignoring it. In the final analysis, their intolerant attitude steered me toward claiming and asserting my difference. Later on, without an African family around, without a husband, and without coercion, I adapted much better to life in Ghana, where I tried to understand the languages, local cuisine, and traditional medicine.

FP So you finally left Guinea, separated from your husband and later divorced. Why didn't you and Mamadou Condé get along?

MC I think we didn't have much in common. When I married him, he was playing the role of Archibald in Genêt's *The Blacks*, a part that did not correspond to who he really was. In the final analysis, I married a kind of mask. Since he is dead, I don't want to speak ill of him, and after all, we did love each other, even if it didn't last. Condé was not Archibald. He did not like to be worried; he feared politics and wanted a trouble-free life. He was a macho man who didn't like having a wife he could not order around. He wanted a quiet wife who would give him kids. He was displeased that I knew all these Marxist militants who were out of favor with the people in power. His reaction was normal, in fact. I understand it . . . now.

FP From what type of family did he come?

MC Poor, and his village was poor too. His mother could neither read nor write. His father died before he was born. Condé went to school through the tenth grade, I think, then became an actor.

FP He must have been theatrically gifted, since his stage presence charmed you. . . .

MC All I know is that when we met, he was extremely good-looking. He was handsome in a Malinke sense: very tall, with a long neck, a beautiful head, and a superb gait. I feel sad now when I think of him. He was one of the people who did not gain anything from independence. Artists were not important in revolutionary Guinea; there was no place for them. I saw Condé completely destroyed by Guinea.

FP When you married Mamadou Condé, didn't he symbolize this Africa where you were searching for roots and a heritage?

MC No. When I married him, he embodied an African type of beauty and nobility in his ways. In fact, our marriage was based on a misunderstanding. It was normal that all of this would end in divorce.

FP Were you a bit annoying for him? This West Indian woman who argued about everything, wasn't she bothersome for him?

MC In his opinion I talked too much and asked too many questions. Sometimes I wonder why we got married. I think it was like people who marry at twenty: love at first sight, sexual attraction, and that's all. I tried to idealize all this, but once the physical interest dulled, there was nothing left.

FP Let's go back now to your geographical itinerary. Why did you choose to go to Ghana after Guinea?

MC One of my friends had gone to Ghana and sent me a note denouncing the socialism of Sékou Touré as a delusion, while praising that of Kwame Nkrumah. That's why I landed with my children in Ghana, where I stayed from 1964 to 1966.

FP Would you talk about your experience in Ghana?

MC I can say that it was much more interesting than in Guinea. I taught French at Winneba, Nkrumah's Institute for Ideological Training. I had very interesting students. Socialism as practiced in Ghana was perhaps not true socialism either, but there was a genuine effort to educate young people as well as the masses. We worked in teams and wrote textbooks adapted to Ghana that did not bear the imprint of colonial ideology. I saw a number of leaders who came to speak to the students, among them Malcolm X and Che Guevara. I saw Kwame Nkrumah several times. In Ghana I started to reflect more deeply on Africa, its reality and myths, the future and problems of socialism. I also had very good friends among African militants in exile in Ghana. I met Agostinho Neto, who had just been freed from prison in Lisbon, Amilcar Cabral, and Mario de Andrade.

FP Had you met Stokely Carmichael or Myriam Makeba in Guinea?

MC They were not yet living in Guinea. They went there much later, around 1969, I believe.

FP So Ghana represented the second phase of your political awareness concerning Africa?

MC I arrived in Guinea in the midst of a counterrevolution. I left shortly thereafter, which means that I did not have time to investigate things deeply. In Ghana I started to grasp the interplay of power and conflicts in a newly independent country. I must say that I was perhaps more mature in Ghana. I had grown.

FP You no longer had a mythical dream about Africa?

MC As I said, I had lost that dream a long time before. I began to see things more clearly, with a true knowledge of what Africa was. But at the same time, I was fascinated with Africa's past. I went to Kumasi to see the remains of the ancient Cape Coast Ashanti kingdoms. In fact, my stay in Ghana was the most fruitful and successful period of my life in Africa. I started to understand why independent African nations functioned with such difficulty. I also came to know people from other areas of the Black Diaspora: English-speaking West Indians, Brazilians, African-Americans. . . .

FP After leaving Guinea, didn't your children suffer by being separated from their father? Were you able to compensate for his absence?

MC One never knows, but I never heard them complain about it. Back then, African fathers didn't spend much time with their children, especially when they were so young. In Guinea, the children would see their father only in the morning at breakfast. They hadn't enjoyed so much fatherly attention that they would miss it later. A father who would talk or play with them, this they didn't have.

FP As an African man, how could Mamadou Condé allow his daughters to leave?

MC When I left Guinea, he didn't know that I was leaving for good. I told him I was going to spend my vacation in Guadeloupe. But when I reached Dakar, I changed my plane ticket and went to Ghana. In fact, I tricked him when I left. In cases like this, everybody cheats. He came to see us in Accra, where I told him that my decision to leave Guinea was irrevocable. He was probably very hurt, though he didn't show it.

FP Didn't he ever want to take his children back?

MC Yes, he always threatened me with this, but only for the sake of appearances. He really didn't want them back. Later on, I entrusted the children to him so I could resume my studies.

FP You left Ghana in 1966. What were the circumstances of your departure?

MC Unfortunately, Kwame Nkrumah lost power in 1966 and took refuge in Guinea. Since I had a Guinean passport, people took me for a Sékou Touré spy, and one morning I was arrested at home in front of my children. I stayed in prison for only a week, thanks to the intervention of Kwame, a Ghanaian lawyer whom I was going to marry. He knew people in the new government, and I was set free. On a personal level, it was the same story all over again. I was an activist, but I would always find myself in love with men who were absolutely not. I was supposed to be tried in court, but thanks to Kwame, I wasn't. My passport was taken away, and I stayed there for three or five months without a passport. When they returned it to me, they told me I had to leave the country. I was deported.

FP Did you have any contact with political prisoners while you were in jail?

MC No. I was by myself in a room where there was a bed; it wasn't a cell. I think it was the place where they held accused people awaiting trial.

FP This part of your life in Africa was quite eventful, but it allowed you to see and meet exceptional, sometimes tragic, figures. For instance, what do you think of the road taken by Sékou Touré, an apparently honest and dignified militant who turned into a bloodthirsty dictator? Wouldn't this provide material for a historical novel?

MC It would make a very banal novel. Unfortunately, the path he took was not very original. I saw Sékou Touré as did everyone else living at that time in Guinea – a very handsome man wearing white boubous and fezzes, who drove his convertible car himself. When he drove by like this, with no guards, I would rejoice at the idea of true popular power. People clapped when he rode by, and it was quite impressive to see. But he became less and less visible as time went on. Then we no longer saw him at all. He withdrew into a sort of ivory tower until he was completely cut off from his people and no longer knew what was really happening in the country. Sékou Touré impressed me at the beginning, but I never really had an intellectual admiration for him. Besides, he had the bad habit of delivering endless speeches that would last four, six, eight hours at a time. These speeches marched out a lot of clichés about revolution and socialism, which I never considered fascinating. He also wrote very bad poems in French, which he stopped doing on Ben Bella's advice, it seems. His whole clique of Guinean flatterers evidently told him his poems were wonderful, and the unfortunate schoolchildren were forced to learn them.

FP Sékou Touré still seems to be a mythical figure for people such as African-Americans. . . .

MC Yes, but I am not an African-American. The only leader I truly admired was Kwame Nkrumah because he had a certain charisma, a great understanding of politics, and a dramatic flair. He knew how to provide what people expected from a leader. I felt a lot of admiration for him and was quite disturbed when he fled to Guinea under such sad circumstances. Cabral was another political leader I admired. He was more like a buddy to me. We talked a lot about Africa and socialism, and he gave me his view of revolution. I was still very naive politically, yet he never made fun of me. His death caused me great personal sorrow.

FP And where did you go after Ghana?

MC To England. I arrived in London with my children in 1966.

FP Why did you go to London?

MC Because Kwame, the Ghanaian lawyer I planned to marry, knew people at the BBC foreign desk in London. The radio station needed someone for its French-language programs broadcast into Africa, so I worked for the BBC. I would review books, exhibits, concerts, and plays from Africa or related to Africa. I remember seeing *The Lion and the Jewel*, Wole Soyinka's first play. I recall having interviewed Stokely Carmichael, who was passing through London. We spoke about Black Power and racial problems in the United States, a country I did not yet know. My stay in London was to be only temporary, after which I would return to Ghana to marry Kwame. I went back to Ghana as planned but without having been granted a divorce. Condé was not answering my letters. This was around 1968–69. However, after Nkrumah's fall from power, Ghana's problems multiplied. There were tensions, struggles, and factions. Life was difficult. I realized that I no longer had any desire to live in Ghana or with a Ghanaian lawyer. This is why I left for Senegal.

FP Were your children still with you?

MC Yes, always.

FP Didn't they suffer from this wandering?

MC They had to be affected by it, but what should I have done? They were with me. In Dakar, Senegal, I first worked as a translator for IDEP [Institute for Development and Promotion], an organization affiliated with the United Nations. Since I hate translation, this didn't work out, and I applied for a teaching position with the French Ministry of Cooperation. I was sent to Saint-Louis, which I loved, then to Kaolack, which I hated.

FP Why did you love Saint-Louis and hate Kaolack?

MC For me, Saint-Louis is magnificent. It is a sleepy city along a river, where nothing ever happens. It lives off its memories. Kaolack is a town of peanuts – dirty, loud, with no style. But Kaolack held one positive thing for me. It was there, in 1969, that I met Richard Philcox, who would become my second husband. He was teaching English at the high school where I worked. At the beginning it seemed a little bizarre to live with an Englishman, a White man. My life up to then hadn't prepared me for it, but that's how it turned out.

FP What attracted you to each other? You didn't have anything in common, did you?

MC No. At the beginning I believe it was simply the fact that I had just spent two years in England. We enjoyed speaking English together. Richard was a volunteer in a program of technical assistance to Africa. He liked Senegal, whereas I was starting to become seriously disappointed with Africa. Richard liked Africa but did not understand it. Our being foreigners brought us closer together. There was certainly something else, since we find ourselves husband and wife twenty-five years later. When it started, I didn't imagine at all that our relationship would last.

FP But then you decided to leave Senegal. Why?

MC I was really fed up with Africa. There were too many setbacks. I saw myself stagnating in mediocre teaching jobs that came with dilapidated housing, with children who were starting to grow up. There seemed to be no way out and no future. I decided to resume my studies, which meant separating from my children for a while. So I wrote to Condé, with whom I was still corresponding, to ask him to come and get the children and allow me one or two years of freedom to prepare a thesis. He agreed and came to pick up all the kids, even my son Denis.

This separation from my children was dreadful, to say the least, both for the kids, who did not at all feel like going with their father, and for me, who had never left them and could not envision life without them. It was very hard, but I did it.

I reached Paris in 1970 and started to work at Présence Africaine. Mr. Kala-Lobé and I were in charge of the *Présence Africaine* journal as well as colloquia. We would select articles and edit the journal's issues. It wasn't a bad job and it allowed me to meet a great number of people. Most important, I registered at the university to prepare a *thèse de 3ᵉ cycle* [thesis] in comparative literature under Professor Etiemble on the stereotypes of Blacks in West Indian literature – in other words, the images of Blacks in the works of West Indian authors.

FP Which stereotypes of Blacks did you discover?

MC Blacks were always depicted as victims. They were also portrayed as spontaneous, sensitive, and in tune with nature. I called into question Négritude's "Negro." That's when I discovered writers such as Michèle Lacrosil and Suzanne Lacascade and realized that women were offering a more striking and critical portrayal of West Indian society.

FP In a 1983 article, "Parlez-moi d'amour" (Speak to me of love), which I read in *Autrement*, you quote Frantz Fanon, who thought that the love of a Black woman for a White man was relegated to the rank of a shameful disease. But he married a White woman, which is in itself a contradiction. In that same article, you mention the reaction of a militant from Mali who thought the love of a leftist Black woman for a White man amounted to ideological treason. You married Richard Philcox, an Englishman. How have people reacted to you, a person who was aware of African political reality, who discussed and debated about it, yet ended up committing conjugal treason with the White "enemy"?

MC Nothing has changed so far. I think racially mixed marriages are seen as betrayals. We women are the great betrayers of the Cause and the Race. Last year, in Guadeloupe, I was attending a film festival with a friend who also is married to a White man. A man stood up and shouted at us: "Why is it that all the important women in Guadeloupe are married to White men?" I believe that I have a personal quality, which is that I don't care at all what people think of me. I felt happy with Richard, and I was not going to leave him because of people's reactions. What bothered me was that my children had difficulty accepting him at first. A White stepfather was hard to take!

FP In that same article published in *Autrement*, you suggested that a Black man, because of certain insecurities deriving from historical circumstances such as slavery and colonialism, would have a hard time accepting his wife's literary success and professional activities, whereas a European man does not have this problem. Is this why Josephine Baker, Simone Schwarz-Bart, Maryse Condé, and others married Europeans?

MC I can speak only for myself. I did not really choose to marry a European. For twelve years I lived with a man who happened to be European, then we got married. Before Richard, I had married an African and almost married another one.

FP You never married or almost married a West Indian man?

MC No. Since I had left the West Indies at an early age, I did not know many West Indian men. I recognize that Richard tolerates me perhaps better than other men, and he does not feel a rivalry with me. He accepts the fact that I have an independent career. The machismo of Black men might not have allowed all this.

FP Because of a sense of insecurity?

MC Maybe. I cannot psychoanalyze them. I have West Indian male friends and see them cheat on their wives and play macho. I consider their attitude toward women totally infantile. I am sure that some of my West Indian male friends would have had a hard time tolerating a woman like me, who has an independent career, writes, and is known left and right.

FP I heard you say once on French television that all men are children.

MC Yes, I think that White or Black, all men are children. A woman's relationship with men is always maternal: she must constantly comfort them, tell them that they are very strong, very handsome, and very intelligent. I believe that all men are like that. They need a certain strength that women provide to them. It may be even worse in West Indian circles because of the way women educate men. Girls hardly count, but boys are revered as little gods. Their mothers must do everything for them. Their sisters do everything for them. Boys don't even learn how to set the table. There are a lot of boys in my brother's family. I have noticed that in his home, girls are considered the boys' maids. I think West Indian women tend to treat their sons like supermen and gods, so their men remain dependent on women for the most basic life necessities. I am not the first person to notice this.

FP Do West Indian women perpetuate their own victimization?

MC It has long been proven that West Indian women, because of their upbringing, repeat patterns that victimize them. However, I can see that things are changing now.

FP Does your racial difference create occasional tensions between Richard and you, or does it strengthen your bond?

MC I don't even think about it anymore, because I have come to realize that all that color business is meaningless. In the final analysis, to marry a Black or a White man does not mean anything. You must simply marry someone with whom you feel comfortable, whatever his color. It is so rare and difficult to get along with a man for any length of time that you shouldn't rack your brains because he is not of the same color.

It is totally passé to divide the world constantly into black and white: "Blacks are good and Whites are evil; Blacks are victims and Whites are henchmen." There are victims and oppressors in both camps. People must develop a new approach to the world and look at it in a new way. Race and color questions have become secondary for me.

FP And what happens when you are in the United States?

MC For historical reasons, which I can fully understand, African-Americans continue to divide the world in two. Given my present perspective, it is almost impossible for me to become part of Black circles in the United States. For example, at Berkeley, where I teach, my social contacts are mainly with colleagues in the French Department. For me, culture and language have surpassed issues of color.

FP Let's go back to Paris, where you were preparing a thesis. What year was that?

MC 1972.

FP Where were Richard and your children then?

MC At first Richard went back to England, but we soon realized that we had to be together. He joined me in Paris, where Denis came in 1973 and the girls in 1975. In the meantime, Portuguese mercenaries invaded Guinea, communications with the country were cut off, and I had not received any mail from there for at least a year. It was very hard. Eventually, my daughters left Guinea with their grandmother and took refuge in the Ivory Coast, where their father was already living.

FP Had Mamadou Condé become politically undesirable in Guinea?

MC No, but he couldn't live there any longer. That country was hell for everyone. People could no longer find anything to eat or drink. There were no cars, clothing, medicine, or money, and government workers were practically never paid. Condé could no longer tolerate this situation. We met in Abidjan to discuss matters, and he gave me custody of my two youngest daughters. We agreed that he would keep Sylvie because she was in eleventh grade, and we thought it better for her to take her *baccalauréat* exams in Abidjan.

FP What did you do back again in Paris?

MC I continued to work at Présence Africaine, but shortly thereafter I started to teach as lecturer at the University of Paris X. Since it was not easy to get a permanent professorship in Paris, I taught in various places, at the University of Paris VII and the University of Nanterre, then joined the faculty at the University of Paris IV on a more-or-less full-time basis, where I taught African and West Indian literature. This is when I wrote *La civilisation du Bossale – Réflexions sur la littérature orale de la Guadeloupe et de la Martinique* (Civilization of the saltwater slave – Thoughts on oral literature in Guadeloupe and Martinique) and *Cahier d'un retour au pays natal – Césaire* (Césaire's *Return to My Native Land*), which is a critical analysis of the works of the Martinican author Aimé Césaire.

FP You also worked for Radio France Internationale. Which topics did you include in your programs?

MC My programs dealt with reviews and discussions of books. I interviewed Francophone authors about their books and would try to analyze them with the writers. All the African writers and several West Indian authors passed through. Some were quite brilliant, like the late Tchicaya U Tam'Si. Others would stammer a bit, but it was always very interesting.

FP You once told me that Francophonie was a political rather than a cultural concept. Could you elaborate on this?

MC It is a way for France to impose the domination of the French language and reinforce its position in certain countries, which automatically become almost French vassals. This is especially true in the case of African and West Indian Francophonie. The West Indies are officially overseas departments of France, so their dependency is a matter of fact. But African countries are also culturally dependent, always awaiting France's opinion of their literary and artistic production. For France, Francophonie is a way to maintain an overseas empire based on linguistic superiority and to strengthen the dependency that can exist between a colony and its mother country.

FP Were the articles you wrote for papers also literary essays?

MC Yes, usually literary criticism.

FP So, after going to France you engaged in many professional activities. What happened with Richard and your children?

MC Richard was a translator for Kodak and provided the financial stability we needed. He had become friends with the children, or at least he had made peace with them, especially with Aïcha. When Sylvie would come for vacation, things would generally go rather smoothly. Yes, I was working a lot, but I think many women do the same when they resume their studies.

FP Wasn't Richard jealous of the time you devoted to your career?

MC Not at all. He was interested in what I was doing, and he has always encouraged me a great deal. I also know how to organize my time. I would work very early in the morning so I could devote myself to the family in the evening.

FP While teaching in Paris you began taking trips to the United States. How did this transatlantic travel go, this triangular "voyage-in-reverse"?

MC Strangely enough, my novel *Heremakhonon*, which had gone practically unnoticed in France – that is, when it was not massacred by the critics – interested people teaching in French departments in the United States, where Francophonie was still unknown. So I was invited to lecture on that topic at several institutions. Then in 1978 I was asked to teach for a trimester at the University of California at Santa Barbara by a West Indian friend of mine who was head of the Black Studies Department there. I spoke very poor English at the time, which turned out to be not very important because the students were mainly concerned with suntans and surfing. There were few Black students. Young men and women with straw-colored hair would come to class half-naked. I read a lot. Since I was thinking of preparing a thesis for the *thèse d'État* [highest French doctoral degree], I was always at the library. I'd never had access to so many books! Richard had taken off from work, and we traveled around California.

FP After this trimester in California, you returned to Paris. How did you happen to go back to the United States?

MC In the following years I was constantly invited, and after the publication of the second *Ségou* volume in 1985, I received a Fulbright award, which allowed me to spend time at a small college in the Los Angeles area. Actually, I didn't really know the United States; otherwise I would not have agreed to spend a year at a small institution. I found chauvinism, racism, and intolerance there in both the White and Black communities, because for them, I was a foreigner, a strange being, a French-speaking Black woman married to an Englishman. As an interracial couple, we frightened people. When the two of us crossed paths with other people on campus, I could see terror in their eyes. Nobody would socialize with us, except for a French couple who were colleagues of mine and were almost as isolated as we were. What's more, I hated Los Angeles, this huge tentacular city where you could only move around by car. In order to get rid of my frustrations, I wrote *I, Tituba, Black Witch of Salem (Moi, Tituba, sorcière. . . Noire de Salem)*, a novel on intolerance and racism. When I left Los Angeles, I swore to myself never to return to the United States.

FP And yet you went back?

MC I went back because it is sort of fascinating to live in the United States. I learned more about the country and now see only its good aspects. The very indifference of people, which hurt me so much before, preserves my freedom. Big universities like Berkeley or the University of Virginia, where I taught later, are places of intellectual emulation and debate. And San Francisco, which is close to Berkeley, reconciled me with the beauty of America. Little by little, I became better known as a writer and my relationships with people changed.

FP After *Segu* was published, you returned to Guadeloupe. Were you thinking of settling down there to continue your career as a writer?

MC Yes, I had written almost exclusively about Africa, and I thought I should write about the West Indies. For a long time I had tried unsuccessfully to return to Guadeloupe to teach at the university or work at a radio station. After *Segu* was published, I was able to come to Guadeloupe without asking anybody for anything. I returned, telling myself that I was going to write and settle down once and for all. But I realized very quickly that this was not possible, and right away I wanted to leave again. Thus, the United States offer came along in the nick of time.

FP Are you going to settle in the United States?

MC Not permanently. I believe we will always be passing through. We will stay there for half or three-quarters of the year.

FP Does being in the United States rather than in Guadeloupe have an impact on your literary output?

MC Living in the United States certainly does inspire me with different subject matters. It also makes me less sensitive to the Creole-French issue, which is a major problem in the West Indies. I become more "marginal" in the context of West Indian literature, but I like it.

FP For the time being, do you feel better in the United States than in France?

MC For me, the United States is mainly a place to work, where I earn a good living. I have many friends there now. What's more, Richard likes the United States a lot, and it is important that your husband like the place where you live. I cannot compare France to the United States. I know France very well and really like being there in spite of my political convictions. I've always known Paris and I feel at home there, whereas I truly feel I'm at the other end of the world in the United States.

FP Let's look at another topic. Has your being a woman been detrimental to your career as a writer?

MC Quite the opposite. It helped me a lot because people were curious to see what a Black woman had to say, what she was thinking. Publishers never refused to read my manuscripts to see what I might be writing.

FP I asked you this question because some African-Americans say it is difficult to be a Black woman writer, to face the double problem of sexism and racism in literary critics and publishers.

MC You know, American women always have exaggerated ideas about everything. That has not been my experience at all.

FP You sell quite a few books. You are, perhaps, one of the few West Indian writers who could earn a living solely by writing. Why don't you do it? Why do you continue to teach?

MC Let's say that I could live off my writing for half the year. I need an additional source of income. Royalties are not really sufficient. I could tighten my belt and earn a living with my writing, but I haven't wanted to.

FP You are the internationally famous writer Maryse Condé. How does it feel to be so well known? Has celebrity changed your perspectives or your way of life?

MC I don't know what people call celebrity, nor do I see how it changes things. Frankly, you do not live your whole life as a famous person. You live with your problems as a mother, a grandmother, and a wife. Nothing has changed on that level. The only new thing is that literature has given me a certain financial independence. I no longer need to beg institutions for work, as I had to do for a very long time. I can now choose to live where and how I please.

FP How do your children and grandchildren react to your being a well-known writer? Has it changed or influenced their lives?

MC This is rather difficult to assess, since one of my grandchildren is six months old and another is three.

FP What about your granddaughter Raki, who is twelve?

MC Raki is pleased, but I don't think it's very important to her.

FP What about your daughters?

MC My daughters are somewhat annoyed at having a mother who is a writer. They are tired of always being known as Maryse Condé's daughters; yet, by the same token, they are very pleased with this recognition. They always introduce themselves with "I am Maryse Condé's daughter." Since they themselves say that, it's maybe a bit hypocritical for them to complain later.

FP What sort of work do your children do?

MC Aïcha is a lawyer, Sylvie is an economist, Leïla has resumed her law studies, and Denis writes.

FP How do your relatives and friends view you now that you have returned to Guadeloupe as a famous writer?

MC My father and mother never knew me as an author because I started writing after they had died. Only one of my sisters lives in Guadeloupe. My brother, who resides in Basse-Terre, Guadeloupe, does not attach great importance to the fact that I am a writer, nor do his children. I am his sister and their aunt, that's all. They read my works but my being a writer is not very important. They never talk about it. I don't have a lot of childhood friends because, as I mentioned, I left Guadeloupe at a very early age. It seems to me that writing or being a writer carries neither prestige nor particular value for Guadeloupeans. To be a writer is simply to be engaged in some strange profession that doesn't really impress people. For instance, what interests schoolchildren is whether it brings in a lot of money. And since I don't ask anyone for anything, live in a comfortable house in Montebello, and don't work in Guadeloupe, people imagine I am a millionaire, which might ascribe value to my line of work.

FP These reactions to the writing profession are not very encouraging. Do they exist because written literature is a rather recent development in Guadeloupe, or because people have traditionally not been encouraged to write? We know, for instance, that slaves had no access to writing or education. But West Indians do value education as a means of social ascent. Isn't this contradictory?

MC Due to Césaire and his influence, there is a literary tradition in Martinique. People there know what writing means, what a writer is, what impact and renown a writer can have at an international level. Césaire, Fanon, Glissant, and Chamoiseau are all Martinicans.

It would appear that Guadeloupe offers an atmosphere less favorable to the development of literature. I do not have an explanation for that. In Guadeloupe people seem primarily interested in political matters. Writers might be more noticed and appreciated if they succeeded in playing a political role (like Césaire) and added some kind of public resonance to their writing. But a writer known outside Guadeloupe, in the United States or Holland for example, doesn't appear to be at all important inside the country. I often go to schools and pose the following question to children: "Do you want to become a writer?" Most of them shrug their shoulders and say: "No, because it's not interesting work at all." They want professions that bring money and power – physician, dentist, airline pilot – or positions that ensure political power, such as congressman or president of the Regional Council. Being a writer is too nebulous for them.

FP How do you react when people see you on the street and exclaim, "Maryse Condé, I read your book. It's wonderful!"

MC In Guadeloupe people know me because they have seen me on television. But I realized at one point that people do not read me.

FP They do buy your books, however.

MC Perhaps, but I repeat: people know my face but are not truly interested in what I do. There's no reaction to what I write, there's no constructive criticism, there's nothing at all. An extraordinary thing happened to me once. A woman came to me and said, "I feel so much admiration for you, I love to hear you, I love to see you, but tell me, what's your name and what is it you do?" I will never forget this. You are some sort of image on a TV screen. Everybody knows you. They say, "Well, she has a nice hairdo today," and "That dress looks good on her," or "That dress looks bad on her," but people don't think about your work or what you are trying to say. What you do have is constant denigration by the majority of the petits bourgeois. A woman I thought was a friend invited me to dinner to tell me all the bad things people were saying about me. I was crushed. She was in utter bliss. For the masses of people, who of course do not denigrate, I am merely a face they saw on TV. When I appear on television in Guadeloupe to talk about my latest book, people ask me afterwards, "So you published a new book. What's the title?" They have not even heard what I said nor know why I was on television. They saw me on TV and that's all.

FP   Do African and West Indian authors write for Europe?

MC   I don't believe so. I write for myself and possibly for those who read my works, whatever their country may be. When you write, you do not write for a particular readership; you write first for yourself, to achieve a certain balance and because you cannot refrain from it. So much the better if what you write coincides with people's expectations, but you do not consciously think of a readership to whom you would dedicate your work. Of course, I speak only for myself.

FP   When you spoke about your return to Guadeloupe, you made me think of a possible foreshadowing in your play *Dieu nous l'a donné* (God's gift to us), in which the main character, Dieudonné, says, "Today, as I return home, I realize that I no longer know how to speak to my people. I no longer know their language, their words of happiness or sorrow" [27]. Do you feel that way in terms of today's West Indies?

MC   I see things a bit differently. I think that for four centuries our people have been victims of political, cultural, and economic domination. Consequently, they are in the process of totally losing their voice. They are threatened. Artists and creators may have the duty to listen to our people before it's too late. In doing this, we may rekindle a pride that they are also about to lose. We may restore their power of speech and imagine what they can be tomorrow. This is the role of creators: not only to preserve the past but also to invent the future.

FP   Like the protagonist in your play *Dieu nous l'a donné*, you thought you would settle down in Guadeloupe. This was a return to the sources and the native land, a theme found in practically all your books. What made you leave the island and come back for only one or two months a year?

MC When you are outside the country, you mythicize it, which is normal. You imagine things and visualize a sort of paradise with lush nature and friendly people. You invent a lot and create something deep down within yourself. But when you come back home, you are faced with the country's reality. You look for what you thought you left behind and don't find it. You quickly become disappointed and frustrated. Then you realize that you must continue wandering. I believe now that it's this wandering that engenders creativity. In the final analysis, it is very bad to put down roots. You must be errant and multifaceted, inside and out. Nomadic.

FP In the chapter Leah Hewitt devotes to you in her *Autobiographical Tightropes*, she speaks of your "criss-crossing of the Atlantic" in real life as well as in your writings [163]. Richard also told me that you were nomads. What are the advantages and disadvantages of such a life? Nomadism may facilitate creativity, but doesn't it also generate problems of alienation? Don't you always feel like a stranger?

MC I now believe that it is good for writers to be strangers to the world and to the various environments in which they find themselves. A stranger's gaze allows for discovery, astonishment, and in-depth analysis. If you are overly familiar with a place or rooted in it, you cannot write truthfully about it. You mythicize. It's a little hard to be nomads, but it's beneficial in the long run. This is strictly my own opinion, of course.

FP In *Heremakhonon*, Veronica also speaks of her nomadism and thinks, "Life is a bitch with a bum leg. . . . She has cast a spell on me and I cannot rid myself of it. That's why I'm wandering from one continent to another, looking for my identity . . ." [Philcox translation, 64].

MC It was negative for Veronica. At that moment in my life I also thought that wandering was negative, but I now think it is beneficial and fruitful. You must wander. I never stop wandering.

FP The majority of your protagonists also travel and lead nomadic lives, resulting in conflicts. When will you give us a well-rooted character?

MC It's not my style. For instance, I don't really see what I could say about the owner of the local bar–grocery store next door, who has never left Montebello, who was born here and will die here. She may be fascinating, but she would interest me only to the extent that she had been in contact with the Other. What interests me is cultural encounters and the conflicts and changes that come from them.

FP Let me ask you a general question now. What are the qualities you most admire in human beings?

MC I like honesty. I hate people who stick knives in your back.

FP What are the faults you detest most?

MC Slander and calumny. I cannot stand hypocritical people who say things behind your back. That kills me.

FP Your characters often feel a lack of love. Do you believe in that feeling?

MC Yes. I believe that love is the only feeling that makes life bearable. Since everybody seeks to share love, it's not easy to find. When you experience it, you should rejoice.

FP Are you a feminist?

MC I have been asked this question a hundred times, and I don't know what it means exactly, so I must not be a feminist. If you ask people in the United States, they probably will tell you that I am not.

FP Perhaps being a feminist means to demand equal status for women and a valuation of their position in society, literature, politics, and everyday life.

MC That depends. I know a Caribbean women writers' organization that meets every two years. Each time they glorify themselves: "What we do is sublime." It is not because you are a woman that you write good books or have essential things to say. There is a danger in believing so.

FP Perhaps women write differently.

MC I don't know about that. In my opinion, a writer is a writer, female or male. It's an individual who expresses herself or himself.

FP How do you use your leisure time?

MC I write all the time, so I don't have that much leisure. I often go to the movies or theater with Richard. I love listening to music, even when I work.

FP What kind of music?

MC Classical or African-American music, blues for instance.

FP I can vouch for the fact that you are a very good cook. . . .

MC For me, cooking is a nice distraction. It is a little like writing: it's creating, mixing stuff, and seeing what comes out. I would not be interested in preparing standard cuisine like everyone else.

FP In 1990 you said in the magazine *Sépia* that writing is "work and a gift of self." Don't writing and self-isolation cut you off too much from political and social events? Isn't it alienating to isolate yourself from everyday realities?

MC I write all the time. I don't do anything else and don't have the impression of being alienated. And since I do not, in fact, write merely amusing tales, I am not prevented from seeing, thinking, and having my point of view.

FP There is quite a bit of irony in your works. Are you an ironic person?

MC The reality of the Black world is so sad that if you don't laugh a little, you can become completely desperate and negative. For me, laughing is a way of looking matters square in the face, of not dramatizing things or falling into a victimization complex or total despair. Fortunately, I am a very ironic person. This saves me, because I have known quite a few tragedies.

FP Doesn't this irony turn provocative in your works?

MC Certainly. I write for myself but also to provoke people, to force them to accept things they don't want to accept and to see things they don't want to see. I think this need to upset people prevails in all my books. Critics miss the essential point if they don't see this. Even *Segu* is meant to rile people, to say things that people so far haven't wanted to see.

FP You disturb your readers, yet they read your works. Are they masochistic?

MC Deep down, some readers like to be told things that are true. They like the truth, a certain lucidity, courage, and honesty. Of course, this is also why a lot of other people do not like me.

FP What is your method of writing?

MC An idea imposes itself on me and I write. I follow the idea and the novel takes shape. The novel itself determines its secondary themes. At least a year elapses between the idea for a novel and its completion. Writing a novel is more work than inspiration. Since it is work, you must write on a regular basis. You can't simply wait for inspiration, because in that case you will never do anything. In Guadeloupe, I try to work in the morning because it is not as hot, but I also work in the afternoon when I live in more moderate climates. When I have things to say, I work hours on end, but when the writing is very laborious, I work, stop, and start again. It all depends.

FP Have you ever been panic-stricken at not finding ideas?

MC Everybody who writes fears not having ideas, not being able to complete a novel. I don't know a writer who doesn't have this fear. It's a constant anguish.

FP Is it easier to write the more you do it, or do you become more demanding?

MC It becomes harder because you have fewer and fewer ideas and are more and more demanding. It no longer just flows, and you have to engage in a more involved thought process. Then, in spite of myself, I think of my readers and wonder, "What are they going to think of it?"

FP Do you make a lot of corrections when you write a novel? Do you rewrite or does everything come to you at once?

MC There are novels that require a lot of corrections because you want to write them in an elaborate fashion. I rewrote *Crossing the Mangrove* (*Traversée de la Mangrove*) extensively, since it was a novel that was rather hard to write, and its style was new to me. *I, Tituba, Black Witch of Salem* was a straightforward novel and easy to write. *Tree of Life* was rather difficult. It all depends on the novel.

FP Are you able to work on several books at the same time?

MC Yes. I have been working on a novel for five years while writing others.

FP Is it easier for you to write plays or novels?

MC Novels.

FP When you write a novel, do you ask friends to read it?

MC No, absolutely never. When I have a problem, I may read a passage to Richard. I also ask him questions that help me find my own answers. Once this is done, I send the manuscript to the publisher.

FP You are both an author and a literary critic. Does one impact on the other?

MC I have not written literary criticism for a long time, at least ten years. I gave it up when I started writing full-time. You cannot do both. At least I don't believe you can.

FP When you write, don't you think about what a literary critic might say?

MC No, not at all.

FP So you don't intervene unconsciously as a critic when you write a novel?

MC No. If you did, you could not write.

FP Do you consider yourself a French, Guadeloupean, or Francophone writer?

MC I see myself as a writer. People who want to add labels are free to do so. I don't live my life as a Guadeloupean or a Francophone writer. I write, that's all.

FP Condé is your first husband's name. Why have you kept it as your pen name?

MC I kept it because I first began to write under that name and divorced only much later, since Condé did not want a divorce. I somewhat regret my name. I was not getting along with Condé when I began to write, and I should have taken back my maiden name, Boucolon, then. But I didn't think about it at the time.

FP Which work by Maryse Condé do you prefer?

MC You always prefer your latest book, since you think it may be a bit better than the others. So, I prefer *Crossing the Mangrove* for the time being. I also like my first book, *Heremakhonon*, because it encountered a lot of setbacks and difficulties. It has been so criticized and denigrated that I have become attached to it.

FP Why has *Heremakhonon* been criticized so much?

MC It was meant to provoke, get on people's nerves, irritate, and run counter to everything that was being said and done. It was written to displease, and I have been rather surprised to see how much it has displeased. The Guadeloupean and Martinican press massacred it. At first, the Africans embarked on a conspiracy of silence; then they attacked the book as well. To this day, African-Americans still challenge me. More than fifteen years after the publication of *Heremakhonon*, people are still debating whether Veronica acted rightly or wrongly, whether she should have had the defense minister as her lover. The level at which people read books never ceases to amaze me.

FP The tone of your first works, was extremely politicized. It seems that this polemical and political tone has diminished in your latest works.

MC At the time of my first works, I was relatively young and militant, whereas I no longer am, in a sense.

FP As you grow older, has your orientation become more humanistic than political?

MC I am more disenchanted.

FP Disillusioned or disenchanted?

MC Not disillusioned – disenchanted. I have observed that things in which I used to believe are not as wonderful as I thought.

FP Does this come from maturity?

MC I think so.

FP What political ideology do you presently embrace?

MC I suppose that when I was young, I was a Marxist, like everyone else of my generation. But I was immediately disgusted with Marxism when I arrived in Africa and saw the horrible things being done by people like Sékou Touré. In principle, Marxism meant a classless society, but there were no societies more hierarchized than those African ones where conflicts reigned between different ethnic groups. For a lot of Africans, a man belonging to another ethnic group is not a man. You can kill him, throw him in jail, do anything to him. That's how Sékou Touré was able to destroy Guinea's entire Peulh population. Moreover, the worship of money and of success at all costs quickly became key words in these new societies. I am surprised that people realized only a year or two ago that Marxism had failed in Eastern Europe. I witnessed a similar failure in Africa long before and wrote about it in *Heremakhonon*. Yet people put this novel on trial, and I was called a reactionary. Without boasting too much, I am proud to observe twenty years later that perhaps I saw things clearly at a very early stage. I no longer have much trust in Marxism, though I hate capitalism. It's a rather uncomfortable position to be in.

FP Do you presently belong to a political party?

MC In Guadeloupe, I share the views of a pro-independence Marxist party called UPLG, the Union Populaire pour la Libération de la Guadeloupe. I am not, however, a card-carrying member.

FP As a writer, what advice would you give to someone who wants to write novels and plays?

MC I would ask that person to reconsider, because it is neither easy nor pleasant work. If the person truly likes it, he or she should go ahead without expecting extraordinary rewards.

FP Or financial success?

MC I do earn a certain amount of money from my books, so I can't complain. But I work so much that it would be a shame if I didn't earn money from them. My books sell well, but this is not the case for all authors.

First Works: Fiction and Literary Criticism

2

FP Maryse, how did you come to literature?

MC Well, I think that I have always written. I remember writing a sort of one-act play for my mother in which she was the only character speaking, responding, and acting. I must have been about seven or eight years old at the time. In high school I wrote for a few small newspapers. As a university student I wrote book reviews for a student publication called *Alizé*, I think. Then in Africa, I took notes that I used later in *Heremakhonon* and *A Season in Rihata*. What I wrote in Africa was too immediate and too personal to be utilized as it was. My experiences had to be considered from a distance and within the peaceful context of literary work. I started to write fiction rather late because I had been busy raising my children. My last daughter, Leïla, was twelve or thirteen years old when I really started to write.

FP Would you summarize your first plays, *Dieu nous l'a donné* and *Mort d'Oluwémi d'Ajumako* (Death of Oluwemi from Ajumako)?

MC *Dieu nous l'a donné* describes the return of an intellectual, a doctor, to a Guadeloupean village. He tries to bring so-called progress to the peasants and finds himself confronted by a local diviner, a *kimbwazé*. This play shows the conflict between tradition and modern knowledge. It says that if people want to do something in Guadeloupe, they must first build upon traditional forces: popular beliefs, traditions, and a certain relation to the occult. In the end, the young doctor is destroyed by various forces that rise against him, especially since he has not managed to establish a dialogue with his people. I wrote the play when I returned to the West Indies for a vacation. I had left there at age sixteen and returned for the first time nineteen years later. Obviously, I had a lot of things to say and write about the country's lack of evolution and change, its eternal poverty and endless political intrigues.

FP   As an epigraph to *Dieu nous l'a donné*, you quote the Martinican poet Aimé Césaire, from his *Return to My Native Land*: "I have wandered long and I return to your hideous, deserted wounds" [70].[1] Does your play take up this theme?

MC   Yes, in a way. All West Indians seem to write about this topic when they return home after completing their studies elsewhere. They are amazed to see that no progress has been made toward political or intellectual liberation and that the country is still deadlocked. They can't avoid talking about it.

FP   Why did you choose *Dieu nous l'a donné* as the title for your drama?

MC   It is a play on words based on the protagonist's name, Dieudonné, which literally means "God's gift" or "God-given." He said the island of Guadeloupe would always be his homeland, whatever its levels of mediocrity and poverty.

FP   Is the use of slang in this play a form of rebellion?

MC   Yes, I believe it is. There is also a lot of slang and crude language in my novel *Heremakhonon*. At the time, this was a way for me to subvert French, assert myself, and break conventions.

FP   The preface of your play *Dieu nous l'a donné* was written by the Guadeloupean author Guy Tirolien, who mentions your "fundamental misogyny" [7]. How do you react to this criticism? Can we speak of misogyny when the writer is a woman?

MC   The play's female characters are somewhat negative, but I believe he was thinking primarily of my way of relating to the island – a negative rapport with the country and the island as a womb. I believe this is what he meant.

FP   Do you accept this kind of criticism?

MC   In general, I accept all types of criticism. I don't intervene. Tirolien

1. Translation by Ellen Conroy Kennedy in *The Negritude Poets* (New York: Viking, 1975).

was a very good friend, a person I liked a lot. He often reproached my lack of optimism because he was a very optimistic writer. He believed in tomorrow, Africa, and the future of Black people. Since this was not exactly my case, he accused me of being pessimistic. You have to consider the term *misogynous* within this context, as part of his broader reproach of me.

FP What about *Mort d'Oluwémi d'Ajumako*?

MC This play's theme was inspired by an event I learned about in Ghana. A traditional Nigerian chief was supposed to commit ritual suicide after twenty years of rule, but one chief refused to comply. He believed that these things should no longer be practiced in modern Nigeria. The whole country was agitated and newspapers wrote about it. People wondered, "Does he really have the right to refuse ritual suicide?" In the end, while everybody was discussing the matter and writing letters to the parliament, the chief died from a mysterious disease, a fever that couldn't really be diagnosed. For me, it was an extraordinary story: here was a man who refused to commit suicide but who was seized by death nonetheless. Perhaps this meant that the gods had decided he must disappear! The story struck me so strongly, as it did everybody at the time, that it inspired me. I changed it only slightly to comply with dramatic requirements.

FP So this play allowed you to study the conflict between modernity and tradition, which is so frequent in Africa?

MC Yes, it allowed me to focus on the reality of history and to see which feudal traditions can actually survive in a modern state.

FP Do you believe Africa's modernization and evolution will occur with or without respect for its ancestral traditions?

MC With respect for its traditions, no matter what happens. I read somewhere an excellent definition of tradition, which said tradition is not static but alive and changing. I wonder whether this conflict between modernity and tradition is not a cliché or a false issue. As Africa "modernizes" itself, it alters and integrates traditions according to its own balance.

FP When and where were these two plays performed?

MC They have been performed often in the past four or five years, which is rather encouraging. They have been staged in Haiti, Martinique, the Ivory Coast, Gabon, and Senegal. When I was in Dakar, I even attended a performance of *Mort d'Oluwémi d'Ajumako* by a young theater troupe called La Compagnie des Tréteaux. I often receive letters from student organizations that don't have much money but that want to stage my plays.

FP Do you prefer the theater or novels as a means of expression?

MC I believe I prefer the novel now. It was so difficult to have these plays performed that I gave up writing drama. They date from 1972–73 but were first performed only in 1978 or 1979. Staging a play requires money, a director with actors, and a place to perform. All of this is costly and makes theatrical expression very difficult.

FP It's a pity because, in contrast to your novels, these plays could reach illiterate people in Africa and the West Indies.

MC Not really, because my plays are in French, so they can't reach masses of people. The notion that theater is better suited for reaching the masses is a myth when plays are written in French and conform to petit bourgeois traditions. This type of theater should be changed, but I am not up to doing it for the time being. In a sense, the novel seemed simpler to me because it acknowledges that it is bourgeois and elitist. Literate people have access to novels. Books are sold in stores and you need money to acquire them. Authors have no illusions. They know they will be read by a limited circle of people that they can almost anticipate.

FP Could you talk briefly about your book *La civilisation du Bossale – Réflexions sur la littérature orale de la Guadeloupe et de la Martinique*?

MC It's a book for students. The students I had at the University of Nanterre, especially the West Indians, said they had access to collections of folk tales but not to any book on oral literature. Since I had given a course on that topic that had interested them, I organized my course notes and reshaped them a bit. I do not specialize in the study of folk tales, so this book represents a modest and unpretentious exploration of the oral tradition, done by me and my students.

FP Afterward you wrote *La parole des femmes – Essai sur des romancières des Antilles de langue française* (The voice of women – Essay on novelists from the French West Indies). Are the message and style of these women writers essentially different from those of men writers?

MC Yes, because they talk about themselves, the difficulty of being a woman in the French West Indies, and the complex relationship between women and men. They discuss the often negative and always ambiguous image that people have of them. What they express is very different from what men express. They don't write about political demands or political consciousness that leads to struggle, nor do they talk about feminism as defined in the West. These women seem interested in matters commonly defined as intimist but that are, in fact, societal problems. They often address color issues and relationships with men and children. They deal more with these matters than with such large issues as racism, exploitation, or ideology.

FP Maryse, you have written essays on West Indian women writers, on Césaire, poetry, the West Indian novel, and so forth. You will remember that at the time of the journal *Légitime défense*, West Indian authors had committed themselves to a functional and non-elitist literature at the service of the West Indian people, literature as communication as well as expression. Do you believe this goal has been achieved in West Indian poetry and novels?

MC I am certain it has not. Writers of all times have dreamed of speaking to the common people. This idea is even more mythical in colonized areas like the West Indies than in countries like France or England. In my opinion, no writer has ever spoken to the West Indian people, because our people do not read. Certain ideas may reach them through newspapers or television. But let's not delude ourselves: West Indians have only a vague idea of novels and poetry collections published in Paris by West Indian authors.

FP At one point Césaire was the hope of the Black world. Has he changed from a "rebel maroon" into an "Uncle Tom"?

MC I am not here to judge him. I admire him the way he is. You have to consider him within the context of his era. Without Césaire we might not be what we are. He was the first to give us racial pride, racial consciousness, and the awareness that the West Indies were not insignificant dots, "specks of dust," in the Caribbean Sea. Of great importance was the consciousness he gave Blacks of their connection to a continent like Africa, where history is so rich and diverse. I think we are all Césaire's children. I consider him to be the Founding Ancestor.

FP Which are the most promising names in French West Indian literature today?

MC I cannot answer your question, because it would seem as if I were passing judgment on people who are all trying to express themselves in their own ways.

FP Have you ever attempted to write poetry?

MC Never.

FP Why not?

MC Poetry has never seemed suitable for me. I am too ironic and caustic, not lyrical at all.

FP What does the title of your first novel, *Heremakhonon*, mean, and why did you choose it?

MC *Hérémakhonon* means "Wait for happiness" in Malinke. *Makhonon* is a verb that means "to wait for" and *héré* means "happiness." When I was in Guinea, there was a department store with that name. In theory, this store offered everything people needed, but it had nothing except Chinese toys of poor quality. For me it was a symbol of independence. I found out much later that Hérémakhonon is also the name of a Malian city where Samori is said to have fought. When I chose *Hérémakhonon* as the title of my novel, the name merely symbolized for me all the illusions fostered by the newly independent African nations.

FP So there was some sarcasm in your choice of title?

MC More disenchantment than sarcasm.

FP Why did you use as *Heremakhonon*'s epigraph this laconic sentence from Pascal's *Pensées*: "Je crois volontiers les histoires dont les témoins se font égorger" (I readily believe stories whose witnesses get their throats slit)?

MC Because Veronica, the story's narrator, doesn't get her throat slit. She returns to Paris, probably reunites with her former lover, and resumes her previous life. She is not the one who dies. She talks about someone who died. Therefore, how valid is her testimony? I wanted to cast some ambiguity on Veronica's testimony and say that it had to be considered cautiously or interpreted in several ways. What is the value of a voyeur's testimony?

FP Could you briefly summarize the plot of *Heremakhonon*?

MC Briefly? It's the story of a young woman who goes to Africa on an initiatory quest, realizes she has no place there, and ends up leaving.

FP So it's a novel about failure?

MC I don't know whether it is a novel about failure. Veronica went to Africa seeking something and did not find it. But she found something else, which she was not looking for. There is no complete failure or total success; you always find something worthwhile in all the steps you take.

FP What did you want to express in this first novel?

MC When I wrote *Heremakhonon,* there was an oversimplified militancy in the air, along with a devout faith in African socialism and the mythification of that ideal. These things exasperated me and seemed quite naive. I wanted to write a novel that would counter what was said at the time with too much superficiality. Basically, I wanted to express how much I had been wounded by everything I had seen in Africa and to point out how difficult it was to build a nation. *Heremakhonon* was a novel about disenchantment and pain. I have been sadly amused by some of the interpretations given to it. People have said, "Deep down she is alienated, she must have sold out to the reactionaries" and so forth. *Heremakhonon* was not fictionalized autobiography at all. It was a novel of protest.

FP But it does include some autobiographical elements.

MC The whole section on childhood and the family milieu is true to life. These are things you don't invent. Also autobiographical is the portrayal of West Indian society in terms of the important Blacks, the ones who see themselves as a high-class Black bourgeoisie but who are, on the whole, terribly alienated. These are the only people I saw during my childhood. They are proud to be Black, but they don't even know what it is. In the final analysis, to be Black, for them, is to act like a White person, to become "whitened." This whole section is truly autobiographical, whereas the rest of the novel contains little autobiographical material – the strike, Birame III's disappearance, the character named Saliou, whom I knew and who died in jail. I never met Ibrahima Sory, the minister; truly a pity!

FP Veronica goes to Africa with an outstretched hand. What does she hope for, exactly?

MC I think she was terribly narcissistic. She thought people were going to take an interest in her but realized they didn't have time for her because of the enormous political problems to solve and the concern about their own survival.

FP The novel is written in the first person. I am tempted to ask whether you are Veronica.

MC I first wrote *Heremakhonon* entirely in the third person. But when I read it over, something didn't click. I had not succeeded in giving it the impact I wanted it to have. It was both a forged confession and false evidence. So I rewrote it entirely in the first person. I think this proves Veronica is not me. (Or is it the other way around?) But it would also be wrong to assert that she is not me at all.

FP Veronica is also a very ambiguous character. She is a woman who seeks her past and her identity, yet she participates in neocolonialism by working for the French system of Cooperation and Technical Assistance.

MC Yes, but this is not the most serious issue. People have to work, and besides people can do a lot of positive things within the context of the Cooperation. I know of examples. What's more serious is that after arriving in Africa, she does not know how, or is unable, to choose her camp. Although she really likes the director of the institute where she works, a politically committed man, she falls deeply in love with one of the pillars of the regime. That's where the problem lies. People think that friendship and love should be subordinate to political options. Veronica wants to be free – that's the crux of the problem. When I think about it now, though, I realize that I was speaking about myself, a person who has never been able to love militants. So Veronica, who is she?

FP Veronica is quite ambiguous in her experiences of love. Through Ibrahima Sory she frees herself from West Indian mimicry of the West, because he represents for her a "nigger with ancestors" [30], the ancestral Africa with which she wants to connect. Sory frees Veronica, as did her former lovers, Jean-Marie and Jean-Michel, in a way. Yet in these three cases Veronica is said to feel like Marilisse, a slave to love, or more precisely, to the condition of being loved. Isn't this deeply contradictory?

MC I used the character of Marilisse, whom I found in history. She was a Negro slave who lived with a White man and bore his children. Through her, I wanted to stress simultaneously Veronica's wish to be liberated and her submission. The trap into which she has fallen is that she seeks liberation through a man.

FP In Ibrahima Sory's comments and those of other characters [Philcox translation, 51, 66, 99], you seem to imply that amorous feelings and the analysis of them are more Western than African. Is the way people express love in Africa very different from that in the West? Is love in Africa more community-oriented than individualistic?

MC You could consult Denis de Rougemont's book *Love in the Western World* (*L'amour et l'Occident*) about this. It has been practically proven that what we call love is a Western creation that first appeared as courtly love. This unreasoned and irrational feeling, binding two people and considered stronger than life or death, is a Western invention. What is important in Africa is to live in harmony with one's community. If you give greater importance to the collectivity than to individuals, obviously there is no room for individual love. Likewise pleasure, sexual enjoyment, and eroticism are concepts that people do not readily discuss or even acknowledge in Africa. I was married to an African man, and I can affirm that the idea of tenderness is expressed so seldom that it seems unknown. At least this was the case while I was there. Times may be changing.

FP In *Heremakhonon*, Veronica says: "I came to seek a land inhabited by Blacks, not Negroes. . . . In other words, I'm looking for what remains of the past. I'm not interested in the present. Beyond that, I am seeking the Oba's palace, the carving on their masks and the songs of the griots" [56]. Aren't both this noncommitment to the present and this quest for a mythical Africa dangerous?

MC The novel is not a handbook telling you what to do, and none of my books should be considered as such. I am not offering lessons. I show people who live their own lives, with experiences that are happy or unhappy, that end the right or the wrong way. Noncommitment may be dangerous, but this is not my problem nor is it Veronica's. She simply expresses what she feels.

FP You don't feel any sense of reponsibility?

MC For what? If people don't want to read my books, they shouldn't. If they don't like what I write by page 10, they can close the book and forget about it. I'm not here to teach people how to build their lives. I am building my own as I go along, without a set direction or predetermined idea.

FP Infirmities are often mentioned in *Heremakhonon*. Veronica thinks: "I am an invalid . . . seeking therapy" [28–29]. What illness affects her? A quest for identity?

MC Yes, it is a quest for identity.

FP The narrative style of your novel, in which there is a constant shift in time and space in order to reach a cultural matrix, reminds me of Michel Butor's narrative strategies in *The Modification*. The climate of uncertainty in your novel forces an active participation on the part of the reader. This is also found in the "nouveau roman" and postmodernist writers for whom everything is constantly changing, without dogma or absolute certainty. Do you place yourself in one or the other of these literary currents?

MC I don't believe writers situate themselves in a particular current. They are placed in it. These shifts you mention were required by the very composition of the book, which describes a woman who is always seeking her own identity and speaks of her former world, the West Indies, and her current world, Africa. I made a narrative choice and don't know whether I was influenced in that respect.

FP *Heremakhonon* contains several remarks on the current situation in Africa. Veronica thinks about the "African avatars of Marxist doctrine" [20], then says of Mwalimwana, "He has realized that socialism will kill Africa" [76]. You speak about Black people's participation in their own oppression, about oligarchy and the like. All of this is quite pessimistic. In the final analysis, what therapy will allow Africa to assert itself?

MC I have no idea. It would be too presumptuous of me to claim that I have solutions. I notice certain things and I am not the only one. Things are going poorly in Africa. In the name of socialism, the same oppression of the people continues. I have said this, and I am not the only one who thinks that people should meet, reflect, and decide whether they really want Africa to change and progress, or whether they simply want things to stay the same. All this can come only from a collectively generated plan.

FP A discussion not necessarily held within the context of Marxist socialism?

MC It might be, but it would be too easy to decide individually and say what should be done. The situation is terribly complex and requires everybody's thoughts.

FP Does the title of your second novel, *A Season in Rihata*, have anything to do with the title of Césaire's play *A Season in the Congo*?

MC The title of my first novel, *Heremakhonon*, was partly blamed for its failure. With the second book, publishers wanted to wink at Césaire and perhaps also at Rimbaud, who wrote *A Season in Hell*. They thought it would help the book, but it was an error in judgment.

FP How would you summarize *A Season in Rihata*?

MC A West Indian woman, Marie-Thérèse, lives in Africa, where she too fails to find her place. She finally does, but only after enduring very cruel rites of passage, including the death of a man she passionately loved.

FP Where does the plot unfold?

MC It takes place in a country very reminiscent of Zaire that is ruled by someone resembling Mobutu.

FP The plot of *A Season in Rihata* is based on a husband-wife-lover triangle, with postindependence Africa as a backdrop. It seems to be a typical bourgeois novel. Weren't you telling me the other day that West Indian writers should innovate?

MC For me, to set a bourgeois triangle in an African context is innovative. Theoretically, there are no sentiments in Africa; thus there are no books focusing on love and adultery. African novels most often describe communities and their problems. I chose to speak about flesh-and-blood characters within a revolutionary context: people who had sex, made mistakes, and betrayed one another. The intrusion of a psychological drama, even a classic one, as you mentioned, into an African environment was, I shall repeat, innovative for me. This is why that book did not please some people, many people in fact. I even heard criticisms stating, "Two brothers in love with the same woman! This is not possible in Africa. It never happens." The things you hear!

FP Did you write *A Season in Rihata* to provoke people, as you said about *Heremakhonon*?

MC To a much lesser extent. I was mainly interested in this female character who couldn't define herself, then finally did, but at what price!

FP People have compared Marie-Thérèse to a sort of Madame Bovary living in Africa. Was she as bored as Madame Bovary?

MC Yes. I was also very bored in Africa.

FP But Marie-Thérèse was not you?

MC She may have been a little.

FP Like *Heremakhonon*, *A Season in Rihata* is a novel based on political metaphors that ends with a failure. What did you hope to achieve with this second novel?

MC In *Heremakhonon* I gave an initial point of view, which was rather impassioned and biased. At the time of my second novel, I had the feeling that I had not shown enough that some forces were working to change Africa. Even if the situation looks hopeless, a lot of things are happening. Some people rebel, some people fight. If this often results in deaths, at least attempts were made to overturn the political situation. I felt this had not been clearly said in *Heremakhonon*.

FP Is the novel based on particular events?

MC You just have to look at the newspapers. I think that almost all the events in that novel, if you study it closely, took place at one time in the Zaire-Congo area, a region I already mentioned to you.

FP *Heremakhonon* and *A Season in Rihata* have heroes who in fact are antiheroes. They appear to be carried along by events and are victims of circumstance. Is this your view of life?

MC If you look at the world around you, you realize that there are no heroes. At least you rarely meet them. I have always met people who tried to do things, though sometimes they did not succeed. Most of the time they were a mixture of strength and weakness. I don't know any heroes.

FP In *A Season in Rihata* Christophe goes in the opposite direction from *Heremakhonon*'s heroine. Veronica seeks her identity in Africa, whereas he looks for his in the West Indies. Will your next novel also focus on a quest for identity?

MC Nobody really knows what his or her next novel will be. I think that a novel is written in spite of you or almost against your will. You don't write a novel saying, "I am going to write about an initiatory quest." After the novel is written, people analyze it and define it as an initiatory quest. As for writers, they tell stories. I belong to the old school and do not believe in the lucid and technically minded writer. I "am written."

FP In *A Season in Rihata* the narrator asks regarding young Christophe, "But how can you become a man when you don't know your past?" [Philcox translation, 27]. This sentence could be applied to a lot of realities, particularly the West Indies. Is there a West Indian identity?

MC I hope so, but it is not my role to define this identity because I don't know it very well; I am not presently immersed in it.

FP The heroines in *Heremakhonon* and *A Season in Rihata* are seeking their identity. Is Maryse Condé to be found in these two alienated West Indian women?

MC Certainly. I assume my alienation.

FP The absurd and alienation are omnipresent in both your novels. Were you influenced by such writers as Malraux, Sartre, Camus, Beckett, or by the theater of the absurd?

MC No, I have read little by them, except for Sartre, of course. I don't believe they influenced me. However, when I was little I read and reread *The Weakling* by François Mauriac. The story of this little boy who committed suicide along with his father fascinated me, and I felt very moved while reading it. Among French writers, I like Marguerite Duras and Modiano. I was influenced primarily by American and British writers. I like the way they write, without emphasis, without a pile of images serving as a screen between the reader and the work. I like the rather precise way of saying things and the plain descriptions, as well as the somewhat cruel and slightly vulgar elements found in North American literature, where people are made to talk the way they express themselves in real life.

FP Which writers have influenced you?

MC A number of them: Philip Roth, Faulkner, Styron, Norman Mailer, and Graham Greene influenced me with their way of telling a story and depicting a particular world. I have also discovered Latin American writers such as García Márquez, Borges, Fuentes, Paz, Puig, and Cortázar, but they have influenced me much less than North American writers. I also very much like the Japanese writers Mishima and Kawabata.

FP How were your first two novels received in France?

MC They went almost unnoticed. There were very few reviews, though rather favorable ones, especially of *A Season in Rihata*. I recall that Jerome Garcin defended it on the radio program *Le masque et la plume*. But that's all. Magazines such as *Jeune Afrique* and *Afrique-Asie* royally ignored them. A friend told me that *Afrique-Asie* had even refused to publish his article on *Heremakhonon*. Neither of these two novels was "politically correct."

FP What happened in Africa and in Guadeloupe?

MC In Africa, apart from a moralizing article by a friend, Bernard Zadi, in *Ivoire Dimanche*, there was the same conspiracy of silence. However, the word-of-mouth system worked, and I was labeled as a person who detests and says bad things about Africa. I was tagged a reactionary. But in the West Indies, critics really broke loose. An article in *Le Naif*, signed by someone whose name I will not mention, called me "a voyeur and a whore," added that "an odor of sperm could be smelled" in the book, and ended up comparing me to Mayotte Capécia. Instead of laughing about this, I cried.

Segu: Grandeur and Decline of an African Family

MONTEBELLO, GUADELOUPE, JULY 6, 1991

3

FP An important stage in your career as a writer was the publication of the two volumes of your novel *Ségou* in 1984 and 1985. Could you summarize it in a few sentences?

MC It is the story of a family over three or four generations, from a time when the Bambara kingdom was stable until it fell into the hands of the French and became a part of the Sudan. It depicts the grandeur and decline of an African people symbolized by a specific family.

FP The family is that of Dousika Traoré and his sons. In the past you were greatly interested in the history of Ghana. Why did you choose to locate this novel in Mali?

MC I had gone on a research trip to Mali and then vacationed there. Richard and I sailed down the Niger River twice, from Gao to Koulikoro, and I was fascinated by all the cities I didn't know and by the entire river culture. Later on, when I decided to write a novel, this area, which I had liked a lot and found beautiful, imposed itself on me.

FP When the English translation of the second volume, *The Children of Segu* (*Ségou – La terre en miettes*), came out, critic Charles Larson wrote a *Washington Post* article [December 8, 1989] titled "A Song of Praise for Africa." Is this appropriate? Doesn't *Segu* speak mainly of Africa's tumultuous past, suffering, and hardships? What did you want to recreate in *Children of Segu* and the first volume, *Segu* (*Ségou – Les murailles de terre*)?

MC A bit of everything: the beauty, the grandeur, the defeats and weaknesses. I did not want to say that everything was beautiful and perfect in Africa. I described what I thought I saw and understood about Africa: the good and the bad, best and worst. *Segu* is not a one-sided, dogmatic novel; it is a novel that tries to show Africa in all its complexity.

FP Your exploration of several generations of the same family is reminiscent of *Roots*, the novel by Alex Haley. Were you influenced by him? Did you read his novel before writing *Segu*?

MC I probably had read the first few chapters. I saw the television production, but *Roots* had nothing to do with *Segu*. I was not influenced by it.

FP How did you get the idea of writing *Segu*?

MC In the course of a conversation, Daniel Radford, then series editor at Laffont's, mentioned that there was no great historical novel about Africa and that one should be written. I totally agreed with him, and little by little the idea of writing *Segu* came to me. It is both a novel I wanted to write and a novel I was asked to write. My idea for the book and my comments on the Bambara kingdom interested them. Laffont offered a contract that allowed me to write *Segu* without spreading myself too thin with other things. It is what people call a commissioned work, but it is also a novel of inspiration.

FP This kind of historical novel requires a tremendous amount of research. How did you go about it?

MC As I mentioned before, after my first dissertation I wanted to write a thesis on Mandingo oral traditions for the higher doctoral degree. As early as 1976 I went to Mali to start my research. As time went by, I realized that I no longer wanted to write a thesis with all that material. The idea of writing a novel was beginning to germinate. With the Laffont contract I gave up the idea of writing a thesis and got absorbed in the novel.

FP How long did it take you to write *Segu*? Do you research at the same time that you write, or do you have very distinct periods devoted to writing and research?

MC I wrote *Segu* rather quickly over the course of two years, but my research began long before.

FP A historical saga like *Segu* is rather fashionable as a genre. Did you write it to please your readership?

MC Yes, since it was also a commissioned work. I followed the rules for that type of novel: coincidences, sensational developments, dramatic turns of events, and unexpected encounters. Like everyone else, I had read Alexander Dumas's works, such as *The Three Musketeers* and *Twenty Years After*, as well as many other cloak-and-dagger novels. In French literature there is a whole tradition of adventure novels with surprise happenings.

FP Did you also plunge yourself into the reading of French epic narratives?

MC I didn't read a single French epic, but I did read a lot of African ones. I read books by Gérard Dumestre, who has written extensively about Mali and the Segu region. I also read works by Kesteloot, Kaké, Monteil, Dieterlen, Amadou Hampaté Ba. . . . The list of everything I read would be too long. I also consulted archives and military reports as well as narratives by missionaries and travelers.

FP When I read *Segu*, I was so confused by the great number of characters that I had to draw a family tree. Why didn't you have fewer characters so that readers could become more attached to them? Why did you include so many characters in your epic?

MC A saga requires lots of characters. Yesterday on the radio program *Caractères*, people were talking about a saga that takes place in Yugoslavia and has seventy characters. The saga novel includes characters that resurface from generation to generation. Even *One Hundred Years of Solitude*, by García Márquez, has a lot of characters. It's a norm for the saga, one of its basic ingredients.

FP It makes reading very difficult. Did you use maps or genealogical trees while writing *Segu*?

MC Absolutely not. While I was writing I remembered the characters.

FP And you wink at people with some of your characters. You use names of people we both know: the Malian writer Alpha Mandé Diarra and the Nigerian filmmaker Ola Balogun. . . .

MC Yes, I have some fun doing this.

FP How do you think up surprise occurrences and encounters between people? Do you use diagrams or do you merely sit down, write, and remember all of this?

MC The narrative takes shape in your head, and the sensational developments are generated by the narrative itself. You are not the one who decides whether a sudden change will take place; the characters themselves create their own dynamics. In a way, the writer merely transcribes.

FP With *Segu* you brought the Malian empire to people who would never have heard of it otherwise. In a sense, you popularized history. Was this one of your goals when you wrote the novel?

MC Not at all. I simply wanted to write a beautiful and moving story. *Segu* was a pretext.

FP Personally, *Segu* allowed me to learn of the existence of Nanny, the Jamaican runaway slave who is a historical figure.

MC I was struck by that character when I went to Jamaica. Later, while I wrote, she came back. I did not make her come. She came on her own. She appeared in the narrative.

FP I remember seeing the statue of a runaway slave, a maroon, in Port-au-Prince, Haiti. He symbolizes dignity and freedom regained. Why does *Segu* describe some Jamaican maroons as traitors and English allies?

MC Because this is also part of their history. Unable to overpower the maroons in Jamaica, the British told them: "We'll allow you the run of the northern part of the island, provided you prevent anyone from deserting the plantations, and provided you bring back all the Negroes who try to run off and become maroons." They agreed and became policemen for the English. It's a fact known to anyone who studies the history, but people don't like to stress that. They prefer to talk about the first phase of the maroons' history, their rebellion. I like to shed light on what people want to hide, and I consider it more important. After the initial agreement with the maroons, the English tricked them anyhow. They imported dogs from Cuba, hunted the maroons, decimated them, and finally deported them to Nova Scotia in Canada. If you tell a story, you have to continue to the bitter end and say that there are two sides to it: one noble and one much less so. In the final analysis, the story of the Jamaican maroons offers a valuable reflection on present times and on power – to see that people who have done everything to gain freedom may be ready to sacrifice others to keep it.

FP In *Segu* there are also a fair number of suicides, which are not frequent in African cultures. . . .

MC Actually, this impression is quite incorrect. I found that women often committed suicide in Africa and that 30 percent of them did it by throwing themselves down wells. Dr. Colomb, a well-known psychiatrist who headed a team working in a Senegalese village, found a fright-

ful suicide rate there and observed that the most frequent way of committing suicide was to jump down a well. Women did this to prevent
members of their community from drinking the well water, thereby
punishing their group and retaliating against it.

FP Why did these women commit suicide?

MC For various reasons: unfaithful husbands, co-wives who cast spells
on them, not having children, and because of the tragedies inherent to
African women in villages.

FP The idea of transgression and curse is present in *Segu* and can be found
in other works. Why do you use this theme so often?

MC Transgression and guilt constitute one of the profound and essential
themes of any literature. If you consider Faulkner, whom I have read
quite a bit, you notice that he depicts many characters affected by a fault
that is not within, but rather outside them, in the community to which
they belong. Human beings are guilty and they don't really know what
they are guilty of. If the feeling of guilt did not exist, I don't really know
what people would talk about in literature.

FP I know that myths of origin interest you within the context of African
cultures. Is guilt an important concept for you because it refers to the
Christian myth of the origin of the world, Adam and Eve?

MC I am not at all Catholic or otherwise religious. I have been strongly
opposed to Catholicism, and therefore it doesn't influence me in the
least. What interests me is the anguish of human beings who are on
earth and don't know exactly why, who wonder whether they are here
for a reason that escapes their understanding, such as a transgression
committed at some previous time. Gauguin painted very beautiful trip-
tychs concerning the origin and finality of human beings. In fact, what
gives a meaning to life is fighting against this sense of guilt by doing
things that can be considered positive.

FP In *Segu*, people refer to Dousika Traoré's transgression, which seems
to affect the future of his family over several generations. What is the
nature of this transgression? Is it his rejection of his ancestors, which is
particularly serious within the context of African cultures?

MC Dousika Traoré is extremely anguished because he doesn't know
which violation of rules he has committed. Can the fact that one of his
children, his eldest son, turns to Islam be considered a fault? Did he fail
to give him enough faith in the ancestral tradition through the education he afforded him? Would he be guilty of that? Or could it be another

grave error committed in his dealings with the king? Some people blame him for not going to war, though he very much likes to receive war booty and wealth. Could he be somewhat of a coward? Could there be an even more serious and older transgression with which he is associated through his ancestors? In the final analysis, Dousika Traoré's anguish comes from his not knowing exactly what he did and, therefore, from his inability to correct his fault, to make precise offerings to this or that god whose wrath has been provoked. It is a way of showing that each human being suffers from a feeling of guilt.

FP Is he affected by a metaphysical guilt?

MC Dousika Traoré doesn't experience his guilt as metaphysical. He simply knows that he feels a tremendous uneasiness with himself, his society, and his family. When he is close to death, he wonders what he did to cause his family to be scattered all about. He questions himself and finds no answer.

FP In *Segu*, Dousika Traoré's four sons are at the foreground of the story, while women are often in the background. Interesting characters such as his first wife, Nya, appear in the story. But very strong women are absent, even though powerful queens have been part of West African history.

MC I was not interested in writing militant and exemplary stories about sword-brandishing women. I saw the African world as it was, with women standing almost always in the background. I simply narrated how things happen in most cases. I am not Ibrahima Kaké, who wrote a series of books in the old days about African women, fetching a queen from here and a female warrior from there. Neither do I want to be like Med Hondo with his film *Sarraounia*. This kind of exemplarity doesn't interest me at all. Things have to be told the way they are. It is obvious that women are, for the most part, oppressed.

FP Don't you occasionally attribute strange feelings to raped women, such as Nabié and Ayaovi, who fall in love with their rapists?

MC No. This reflects a well-known relationship between victims and victimizers. It is reminiscent of Liliana Cavani's films and all the movies on the relationships between women in captivity and Nazi officers; it's a whole thematics. *Segu* is not a militant novel, and until people understand that I don't write such novels, they will not comprehend my writings at all. In an exemplary work, the raped woman would go get a knife and kill the man who raped her. This is of no interest to me. I am interested in what is not conventional, Manichean, or pseudomilitant. *Segu* is not a novel about the liberation of women.

FP   In *Segu*, you also mention human sacrifices that actually took place in the kingdom of Abomey. Haven't you been accused of overemphasizing Africa's past violences and of playing into the hands of those who would discredit the continent?

MC   But I hardly talk about human sacrifices! Once, in passing, an enemy of the Bambaras mentions them. There are two rapes in the novel. Violence is part of history. I invented nothing. People should read, for instance, works by Palau-Marti and Glélé on human sacrifices in the kingdom of Dahomey! In my opinion, if Africans didn't like *Segu*, it was not just because it was written by a non-African woman (although that was part of it – I won't elaborate on other writers' envy, which is unavoidable). It was because the work didn't contain complacency or easy idealizations. I'm inclined to side with Nigerian Professor Onwuka Dike, who said that people must accept Africa's past with everything it includes, human sacrifices and all. That's how you forge an identity. I received a lot of criticism for the way I depicted Islam. *Segu* is based on interviews and archival documents. In some countries Islam created a bond that allowed people to resist French colonization. But at the beginning, in many instances Islam came by fire and by sword. People should see Ousmane Sembene's film *Ceddo* again. What crime is there in stating things?

FP   One of your characters, Omar, tries to resist beautiful Kadidja's appeal and believes he is resisting evil. Did you stay close to historical and sociological truths in attributing to an African Muslim of long ago a view of women as maleficent beings, which is similar to the view prevalent in the Western world?

MC   This fear of the sin of the flesh can also be found in Islam. The Koran says, "If you are on fire, you must get married," which means that if you feel desire for a woman you have to legitimize it immediately by marrying her, and only then is sexual desire permissible. Otherwise, woman is a constant temptation that man must avoid.

FP   *Segu*'s Bambaras seem to be still quite attached to their gods in spite of their conversion to Islam. Is this true today?

MC   All I know is that when I was writing *Segu*, I interviewed people and realized they remained largely animistic, though they were theoretically Muslim.

FP You mix historical reality and irreverent images in this novel. You describe the participation of Muslim merchants in the slave trade, as well as their bloody religious wars and forced conversions to Islam, which are historical truths. But you also depict Muslim faithful who "bellow out" their readings from the Koran or "bleat" like sheep while reciting their prayers. What did African Muslims think of this?

MC They probably hated it, but in *Segu* the non-Muslim Bambaras are talking, not me. I have no opinion concerning Islam.

FP The book could be seen, however, as reflecting an anti-Muslim viewpoint, since it does not describe Christians with the same irony.

MC This is totally untrue. The novel doesn't spare the missionaries in Nigeria. What about Eucaristus's teachers?

FP Didn't people take you to task for denouncing the participation by Africans in the slave trade?

MC Isn't it true that Africans participated?

FP It is an undeniable historical fact. In your view, which has left a more significant imprint on today's Africa, Islam or Christianity?

MC Undoubtedly Christianity in Zaire, but Islam in Guinea. It all depends on the region. It also varies within the same country. Christianity prevails in southern Benin, while Islam dominates in the north. I don't think one religion outweighs the other that much. At one point there were more Muslims, but I believe that Christianity is gaining ground today.

FP How did Europeans react to your description of colonialism and its abuses?

MC I don't know what they thought. I was not the first to describe abuses, nor the last.

FP I felt a craving for more at the end of *Segu*'s second volume. I would have liked to know the fate of several characters. Will there be a third volume?

MC Absolutely not.

FP Why "absolutely not"?

MC Because I have already traveled away from it. My spirit has journeyed to another world. I don't want to go back to telling the story of the Bambaras or Segu. It's over for me. I am no longer interested. You leave what you have done behind and move on to other things. Also, *Segu* was a novel intended for the general reader. I want to experiment with other narrative techniques and writing styles.

FP *Segu* was a very successful novel when it came out. How many copies were sold?

MC The first year, 300,000 copies of the first volume in French and fewer copies of the second volume. It was brought out in twelve countries and translated into a dozen languages: German, Polish, English, Italian, Spanish, Swedish, Norwegian, and others.

FP Do you sometimes work with the translators of your works?

MC No, I never do.

FP How has *Segu* been received in countries such as Germany and the United States?

MC I think it has been well received in Germany. I spent a week there promoting it, and everything seemed fine. Without meaning to boast, I can say that in the United States *Segu* is about to become a classic for African-Americans.

Return to the West Indies and the Americas

MONTEBELLO, GUADELOUPE, JULY 9, 1991

4

FP *Pays mêlé* (Mixed[-up] country) contains two short stories about the West Indies. I understand that you wrote it when you came to settle in Guadeloupe.

MC Actually, I wrote *Pays mêlé* long before I permanently settled here. One of the stories takes place in Jamaica, where I went on a teaching assignment in 1980. I really liked the country. It impressed and interested me a great deal. Later, I went back with Richard on vacation, and that impression was reinforced.

FP What evoked those feelings again?

MC First of all, Jamaica is a wonderful island for its landscapes. It is green and wooded, in contrast to Haiti, for instance. But the part of Jamaica that intrigued me the most is not green nor wooded, but rather barren — Cockpit Country, where maroon villages are located. I bent over the grave of Nanny of the Maroons and walked down small, almost impassable paths that had been closely guarded by the maroons. History is still present there. The Rastafari phenomenon also drew my attention. Thanks to a Colombian friend, I spent two days in a Rasta commune, amidst ganja smokers, trying to grasp the Rasta doctrine and its fascination for people. In Negril, for example, there were hundreds of Americans, who went there, I suppose, to forget about the United States. At the political level, Michael Manley's socialist experiment reminded me, with added violence, of what I had seen in Africa. When I returned to Jamaica with Richard, Seaga was in power and things had changed. Since I was very interested in popular music, we threw ourselves into reggae and attended large public concerts. It was quite exhilarating.

FP What do you think of the Rastas who advocate Black people's spiritual return to Africa through devotion to Ethiopia and to the Negus?

MC I think that their deification of the Negus is strange, but the Rastas I met didn't attach great importance to it. They were more concerned with the total lifestyle: not eating certain things like pork and seafood, not drinking alcohol, and practicing a form of self-discipline and asceticism.

FP This encounter with Jamaica apparently inspired you to write the short story "Nanna-ya" in *Pays mêlé*. Would you please comment on the story and explain its title?

MC "Nanna-ya" means "Long live Nanna" and is the beginning of a song celebrating Nanny of the Maroons. It's a very popular song in Jamaica. The short story talks about a woman who steals the manuscript of a researcher compiling notes on a slave rebellion. For the scholar, the theft of the manuscript meant losing a whole series of myths and phantasms which were actually oppressing him. This loss may allow him to get closer to his wife and resolve problems between them.

FP The theft of a manuscript is, of course, any writer's nightmare. . . .

MC Yes, but I didn't really think about that when I was writing the story. I mainly wanted to show how a dream can distance you from reality. The protagonist was dreaming so intently about his rebellious African ancestor who had led a slave revolt, and he was so eager to write about a mythical past, that he forgot the reality around him. In the meantime, his whole family was disintegrating: his children despised him, his children were leaving home, his wife was unhappy. Only when he was free of the mythical past did he begin to learn to live in the present.

FP The young woman who steals the manuscript had gone to Jamaica in search of her identity. . . .

MC She steals the manuscript because she wants a life. In countries like ours, people will do anything to survive. Some turn to religion, others to politics. She resorts to stealing a manuscript, which she then types, reshapes, and publishes as her own, and it makes her famous.

FP I find it regrettable that, being the daughter of a Jamaican man and an

Englishwoman, she travels from England to search for her ancestors in Jamaica and ends up having to steal them, literally and symbolically, through this manuscript.

MC I didn't think about all of that. I simply saw someone who came home and didn't quite know how to merge into the island society. She tried to use the only obvious means available to a woman, her body. She gave herself to one man, tried to seduce a second and then a third. She is woman as victim, reduced to using resources that may be less than totally noble in order to extricate herself from difficulties.

FP What is the other story, "Pays mêlé," about?

MC It's about a medical doctor who tells the story of a young boy killed by a bomb. He tries to recount the boy's life, along with that of his mother and his grandmother. I don't name where the action occurs, but it's obviously about Guadeloupe. Let's leave it at that.

FP Could you explain the meaning of *pays mêlé*, the title of this short story and the book?

MC In Creole, *mwen mêlé, mwen mêlé* means "I have problems." The word *mêlé* also refers to mixed blood, to people of mixed parentage. *Pays mêlé* is a play on words and refers both to a country with problems and to a country where people are of mixed blood.

FP You make your readers travel all around in your novels. *Heremakhonon* was inspired by Guinea; *A Season in Rihata* takes place in a Central African country; *Segu* occurs mainly in Mali but also in other areas of the Black Diaspora, such as Brazil and Jamaica. *Pays mêlé* speaks of Guadeloupe and Jamaica, and *I, Tituba, Black Witch of Salem* takes us to Barbados and the United States. How did you decide to write this last book?

MC Simone Gallimard, director of Mercure de France Press, once suggested that I write a book about a heroine from my region. I was not interested in the topic and had no good ideas for it. I kept her suggestion in mind, though. Later on, I was doing some research at the UCLA [University of California, Los Angeles] library and came across a book on Tituba, a Black woman who was one of the Salem witches. I was unaware of her existence and asked about her, but I didn't find anything because nobody seemed to know of her. There were historians at the institution where I was teaching at the time, but they didn't know about Tituba and were not the least bit interested in her. So I thought I would write her story myself. Ann Petry, an African-American novelist, had already fictionalized her in *Tituba of Salem Village* (1964), but I wanted to reinvent her destiny. Ann had written a book for children, and I wanted something else.

FP In the past few years, some feminists have rehabilitated witches, whom they see as victims of public humiliation and religious intolerance in patriarchal societies. They view witches as strong and independent women. Did this kind of thought influence you when you wrote the novel?

MC I was not even aware of this feminist point of view. I was simply fascinated by a historical figure.

FP How long did it take you to write *I, Tituba, Black Witch of Salem*?

MC The research period for the novel was very short, since I found practically no documents concerning Tituba. I wrote the book very quickly, in six or eight months, while I was teaching at a small college in the Los Angeles area.

FP The epigraph says, "Tituba and I lived for a year on the closest of terms. During our endless conversations she told me things she had confided to nobody else" [Philcox translation, v]. Here the writer might be seen as a privileged interlocutor. Should we believe that this derives from occult or supernatural literary inspiration?

MC Tituba's spirit did not come to me. The epigraph was just for fun. But there always is a certain relationship between writers and their characters. "Supernatural" inspiration does exist in a sense, since you suddenly feel like writing about a totally imaginary creature whom you have never seen or met, and who doesn't exist. You don't really know why all of a sudden you want to write about this or that character. The very act of writing is "supernatural" in itself.

FP How do you describe Tituba in your book?

MC As a young girl, she was initiated into witchcraft by an old woman called Mama Yaya. On her island of Barbados, Tituba uses powers of the occult to benefit her community. Later on, as a slave in Boston, she tries to do things for the children of her owner, a pastor. Unfortunately, the children misunderstand her. They think she does the devil's work and denounce her. She is put on trial and ends up being sold to someone, we don't know to whom. In my book I imagine that after getting out of jail, she goes back to Barbados and participates in an unsuccessful slave revolt. In the end she is hanged. She joins the world of the spirits and becomes an epic heroine forever present in the island's collective memory and folklore.

What some critics did not understand is that the book is ironic. It is also a pastiche of the feminine heroic novel, a parody containing a lot of clichés about the grandmother, the sacrosanct grandmother, and about women in their relationship to the occult. I split my sides laughing while writing the book. To show how much fun I was having, I imagined an encounter in jail between Tituba and Hester, the heroine of Nathaniel Hawthorne's *Scarlet Letter*. Both talk about feminism in very modern language. Tituba's return to her island, her relationship with the maroons, and the links to spirits who appear and disappear are ironic elements.

FP Your treatment of the occult doesn't refer to the magic realism found in the works of some West Indian writers?

MC Absolutely not. All of this is largely mockery. Besides, I don't see how people could read *I, Tituba, Black Witch of Salem* with any seriousness in the first place and make Tituba into something she is not.

FP So with the character Tituba, you did not intend to denounce the intolerance that existed and still exists in the United States?

MC Perhaps, but that's another story. I was mainly interested in the racism affecting this Black woman, who had been completely forgotten, crossed out of history. Tituba was not rehabilitated, whereas all the other women were. The county archives contain the list of possessions returned to them. We know that some women went back home, but we don't know what happened to Tituba after she left prison. It is believed that she was sold to pay for expenses incurred during her incarceration. All of this seemed revolting to me, and I wanted to give a life to this obscure and forgotten woman. But since I am not the kind of writer who creates model characters, I quickly destroyed what might appear exemplary in the story by rendering Tituba rather naive and sometimes ridiculous.

FP In your book, children are the main accusers of Tituba and the other Salem witches. Did it really happen that way?

MC Children triggered the trial, children testified, and as time passed, some retracted their stories, some contradicted themselves, and some stuck to their charges. People believed them precisely because they were children, and children, as a rule, are thought not to lie.

FP Tituba, "a slave originating from the West Indies and probably practicing 'hoodoo'" [110] is a phrase that surfaces as a leitmotif in the novel.

MC Yes, because that was the charge. I found that sentence in trial
records.

FP References to occult powers are found in several of your works. Do
you believe in the occult?

MC What difference does it make? I don't believe in it, but these beliefs
are still quite prevalent in the West Indies and Africa. I incorporate them
into my narrative plots when it is appropriate. What a writer believes as
an individual does not matter!

FP Tituba, "a slave originating from the West Indies . . ." I have the impression that her status as a slave may have helped her during the trial, if
she said whatever people wanted her to. Was she acquitted because, as a
slave, she was denied freedom and was therefore considered less responsible for her actions?

MC She was not very important; she was an object. Tituba was the only
one to admit that she was a witch, and she could not recant her testimony later. Because of this, she was spared, so to speak, and not exe-
cuted. If only you recognized that you were guilty, the court would leave
you alone. The other women did not plead guilty. Tituba had only her
wretched life as a slave to lose, and she said whatever they wanted her
to. She admitted she was a witch to avoid beatings, mistreatment, and
hanging.

FP *I, Tituba, Black Witch of Salem* has a "John Indian" as Tituba's husband, a totally despicable character. Did he exist in real life?

MC Yes, John Indian really existed. In my research, I found two or three
lines about him, stating that he abandoned Tituba when she was arrested and went to settle somewhere else with another woman.

FP At one point when he is speaking to Tituba, he makes comments reminiscent of Fanon and Genêt. Tituba feels frightened when she meets
other slaves who are John Indian's friends, and he tells her, "Don't put
on such a face, or my friends will think you're condescending. They'll
say your skin is black, but you're wearing a white mask over it" [32].
This recalls Frantz Fanon's *Black Skin, White Masks*. John Indian continues by saying, "They expect niggers to get drunk and dance and make
merry once their masters have turned their backs. Let's play at being
perfect niggers" [32]. This certainly reminds me of a passage from
Genêt's play *The Blacks*. Is this still meant to be ironic?

MC Yes.

FP But did Fanon and Genêt actually influence you?

MC Certainly not in this book.

FP What do you think of them?

MC I like Fanon a lot, especially because he is a wonderfully good writer. *The Wretched of the Earth* is one of the most beautiful texts I have ever read in the French language. The last pages are splendid, with that exhortation to the Third World to start a new history of mankind. It also contains extraordinary pages on national culture. I deeply admire Fanon as a writer, but we should recognize that his analysis of the behavior of West Indian Blacks is dated. His attitude is very macho, and his criticism of Mayotte Capécia is unfair. *The Wretched of the Earth* is less dated than *Black Skin, White Masks*, but it offers no solutions. Fanon provides a very good analysis of the situation in his time by showing the role of the bourgeoisie and of violence. In my view, though, he did not project himself into the future. It is very beautiful and prophetic to say that the Third World must start a new history of mankind, but how? As for Genêt's influence, I have seen *The Blacks* and *The Maids*, but I must admit that I am less familiar with his work.

FP I would imagine that you appreciate the iconoclastic and provocative aspects of *The Blacks*.

MC I saw it in 1960 and have forgotten the details. I mainly liked the way masks were used. It was an innovative way to stage a play. It had a farcical and very cruel side to it. I found that beautiful, I believe.

FP At one point you mix Tituba's fate with that of a kind Jewish man, Benjamin Cohen d'Azevedo, who becomes both her owner and her lover. Did he exist in real life?

MC No, he is a character I imagined after a conversation with a Jewish friend. She gave me documents about the Puritans and pointed out that they too had persecuted Jews – for example, by preventing them from living in certain counties in the United States. I combined Jews and Blacks to establish a link between the Black and the Jewish Diasporas, and to show that the Black community has not been the only one to suffer racism and prejudice in the United States. I felt that this was interesting for the dynamics of the narrative. For the same reason, I mention the common dispossession of Blacks and Indians.

FP At the end of the novel Tituba says, "I knew that . . . America was preparing to dominate the world with the sweat of our brows. I knew that the Indians had been wiped off the map and reduced to roaming the land that once was theirs" [170]. Here again, the fates of Blacks and Indians are associated. Both groups suffered exploitation and dispossession, on which American capitalist success was based. Does Tituba's prediction reflect your own thought? Do you believe that slavery and the long-term exploitation of a free labor force allowed the development of U.S. industrial capitalism?

MC Yes, this is Eric Williams's thesis, which is commonly accepted. I didn't think particularly about this idea while writing the book, but I agree with him.

FP For some time now, Vince Goodwin, an African-American, has asked that the U.S. government pay damages plus interest to all Black citizens in reparation for the harm done to them by slavery. He cites as a precedent the damages plus interest paid to Japanese-Americans for their detention in camps during World War II. What do you think of this?

MC Yes, I have seen this on television. No comment.

FP In *I, Tituba, Black Witch of Salem* you depict the suicide of a slave and Tituba's abortion, which she performs herself. Was this done to intensify elements that can be historically verified? Were suicides and abortions frequent among slaves in the Americas?

MC One of the first things you learn from research on slavery is that slave women killed their children to spare them from a fate like their own. Infanticide was very common on plantations. Father Labat repeatedly mentions this fact about the West Indies. Infanticide was widespread in all slave societies of that era, the United States included. It's also a common theme in literature by Black women, if you know what I mean. . . .

FP In your narrative you create friendships between White and Black women. There is a mutual affection between Tituba's mother, Abena, and Jennifer, the young wife of plantation owner Darnell Davis. Tituba becomes the friend of Elizabeth Parris, wife of the Puritan minister. In both instances Black women symbolize strength and vitality, while White women are quite diaphanous, sickly, and subservient to their husbands. Did the slave-master relationship often generate this kind of affection between people?

MC The Black-White female relationships here underscore stereotypes. On the one hand, you have the pure, ethereal, weak White woman who cannot tolerate hot weather and is sickly. On the other hand, you have the strong, robust Black woman. I don't believe the conditions of slavery allowed for friendships between Black and White women, between slaves and mistresses.

FP At one point Tituba is questioned about her occult powers by three Puritan ministers [90–91]. There is a quasi rape and a vision of horror. You depict people with black hoods who are strangely reminiscent of the Ku Klux Klan. Is this also parody?

MC No, that's true. The only true elements are these interrogations. They are based on historical fact.

FP At the end of your novel, Tituba alludes to hooded men who will appear in the future and inflict torments upon Blacks. Do you perceive a link between the intolerance of the Puritans and the fanaticism of today's Ku Klux Klan, which burns crosses and persecutes people, also in the name of God? Does *I, Tituba, Black Witch of Salem* reflect a contemporary context?

MC This was done to confer a prophetic tone on Tituba's words, since through her I also wanted to talk about present-day America. The history of the Puritans did not interest me as such. I wanted to show that the intolerance, prejudice, and racism that victimized Tituba still exist in contemporary America. *I, Tituba, Black Witch of Salem* is not a historical novel, it's about the present.

FP If that was your purpose, why didn't you address intolerance and racism in a novel set in the present?

MC What about the creator's freedom and pleasure? Writing must also be fun for the writer. Creative writing takes you away from daily life. Writing a novel is not like drafting a propaganda leaflet. It is not a denunciation. Let's leave that to people involved in politics. If I were to talk within a contemporary context about a Black man who was recently beaten up and almost killed by policemen in Los Angeles, it would not be as original, for me and for others, as telling the same story in a seventeenth-century environment and giving it present-day resonance. I think a novel is not a journalistic report. It implies a degree of dreaming and imagination.

FP How do you compare racism in the United States and in France?

MC There used to be less racism in France because Blacks were not very numerous. Today I believe that the average Frenchman is almost as racist as the average American. We heard Jacques Chirac refer to immigrants' smell and noisiness in order to appeal to the French electorate. We hear Edith Cresson wanting to send them back home. Not to men-

tion Le Pen! The way racism is expressed may be different in each country. The United States has ghettos. But if you think about it, you can see
something pretty similar walking around the Barbès neighborhood in
Paris. In my view, both societies are almost equally racist.

FP But racism has never been legal in France, as it was in the United
States.

MC That doesn't mean a thing. Those laws existed in the southern states
and were finally abolished. As in South Africa, people's hearts will not
change overnight. Apartheid is being dismantled, but the country will
long remain extremely racist.

FP I would like to return to Tituba's story. The last chapter of your novel
depicts a slave rebellion in which Tituba and her young lover Iphigene
participate. Tituba asks him, "Do you think we'll win?" He shrugs his
shoulders and answers, "What does it matter! The important thing is to
have tried and to have refused the fatalism of misfortune!" [169]. To try,
to act, and to challenge fate, is this your philosophy of life expressed in
Iphigene's words?

MC I don't know whether I have a philosophy of life that remains constant as I change and grow older. But you may be right. I believe in action
for action's sake. For instance, I am an *indépendantiste*. I am a militant
supporter of Guadeloupe's independence though I am convinced I'll
never live to see it. The awareness of failure must not prevent or retard
action. Quite the contrary!

FP Fate is often omnipresent and omnipotent in your books. Does this reflect your own fatalism?

MC I am certainly not fatalistic. I do my best to portray a given community. In Guadeloupe quite a few popular proverbs say that misfortune is
the Black man's sister and that she never leaves his side, which is a sign
of widespread fatalism. This popular reality inspires me. It's the language of fiction.

FP At the end of the novel, Tituba exclaims, "Yes, I'm happy now. I can
understand the past, read the present, and look into the future. Now I
know why there is so much suffering and why the eyes of our people are
brimming with water and salt" [178]. Has she achieved immanent
knowledge and wisdom?

MC It's mostly an ironic allusion to Jacques Stéphen Alexis's *Compère
Général Soleil*. It's a collage. Those are Hilarion Hilarius's words as he is
dying at the end of the book.

FP Because someone turned her in, Tituba and Iphigene are hanged and die after the slave revolt fails. Slave turning against slave – is this another cliché?

MC We know full well that all the rebellions were aborted. The novel had to have a credible ending.

FP By the way, why did you write this novel in the first person?

MC I don't know. It's the same as with *Heremakhonon*. I must be Tituba. I am the witch!

FP Most of the novel's chapters are about ten pages long, whereas chapter 5, which describes Tituba and John Indian's wedding, and chapter 8, with Tituba's lament for her lost child, are only one or two pages. Why is there such a disparity?

MC That's the structure, the structure of the book.

FP Why did you choose it?

MC You don't choose it. The book writes itself, and its structure is dictated to the writer along the way. The chapter stops when an idea comes to its end. You don't decide whether to write a short or a long chapter; it all depends on what you wanted to show. The chapter stops there or else goes on. You don't really control structure.

FP What is the theme of your 1987 novel, *Tree of Life*?

MC It's the story of the Louis family from the moment when Albert Louis refuses to continue working in the sugarcane fields, turns his back on them, and tries to climb the social ladder. This is not easy; it takes time. Later, when his offspring become petits bourgeois, they realize that this concern for social climbing was totally absurd. They want to go back to the common people but know that it is impossible once you have left them. You could call it the story of a dynasty.

FP Is it a Caribbean *Segu*?

MC No, it's nothing like it. *Segu* is a historical novel, whereas in *Tree of Life* I wanted to play with history and memory. You know that Pierre Nora established the difference between history and memory. *Tree of Life* has a historical backdrop, but the narrative focuses on the collective memory of the Louis family, on what Coco, the family's last-born, is able to reconstruct about events before her birth that will shape the future. At the end of the novel, there is an important passage in which she describes the book she will write one day. It's a sort of public literary statement, my own perhaps. "It would be," she says, "a story of very or-

dinary people. . . . A book with neither great torturers nor lavish martyr-
doms. . . . The story of my people" [Reiter translation, 357]. Henceforth,
history must be subordinated to the process of collective or family
memory. For instance, the book to which the Uncle Jean character dedi-
cates his life, *Unknown Guadeloupe*, is based not on historical facts but
on the memory of Guadeloupe's farm laborers. I could give you many
other examples. The historical characters who intervene in the narrative form only the background for particular events.

FP How did you devise the plot for *Tree of Life*?

MC The novel is broadly based on the history of my own family. It focuses on the barely fictionalized story of my father's son by a first marriage who left Guadeloupe to study in Saumur, France, right after World
War I and began the "mulatto" branch of the family. However, in the
novel, the family account of its origins is interspersed with a great deal
of fiction. For instance, I borrowed the forefather, Albert, from a young
man I met in Los Angeles. This is a quite an extraordinary story. I went
to give a lecture at a university, and a young, light-skinned, red-haired
Black man was waiting for me at the entrance. He welcomed me by saying, "Ka ou fè, Mariz Kondé?" – How are you, Maryse Condé? We went
on talking for a few minutes in Creole. His Creole was better than mine,
and I asked him where he was from. He laughed and told me he was from
Panama. His great-grandfather had emigrated from the French West Indies to work in the Panama Canal construction, and his family stayed
there. As a result, this young man spoke Spanish, English, and Creole
but no longer had any knowledge of French. This story interested me
and we met again. He showed me documents, and I interviewed him
about his grandfather and included that information in the novel. I went
to San Francisco to follow in the footsteps of those who had built the
Panama Canal. There is a museum there about the construction of the
canal. It was fascinating.

FP West Indian participation in the building of the Panama Canal is not
well known.

MC Actually, it is. If you ask four West Indians, at least one of them had a
grandfather who went to Panama. The West Indians came mainly from
English-speaking islands such as Jamaica, which explains Marcus Garvey's visit to Panama in the novel. It's a historical event.

FP Did a lot of these West Indians go back home?

MC Yes, most of them came back pretty rich – that is to say, relatively rich – and became petits bourgeois, somewhat like Albert, the fore-father in *Tree of Life*. Others went to settle in New York.

FP The emigration problem has greatly affected the West Indies. Today people talk about migration to France and its effects on Guadeloupe and Martinique. Can a comparison be drawn between the migration to Pan-ama and the present movement to France?

MC Yes, but I was not really thinking about that while writing the novel. I wanted to show that West Indians move around a lot, though some people incorrectly believe they never leave the islands. In fact, West In-dians have gone all over: to Panama, Africa, Europe. I wanted to show that the West Indies is a place of generation and dispersion, not confine-ment. As I said earlier, some West Indians went to the United States af-ter digging the Panama Canal. The West Indian community in the United States was very large by the time Marcus Garvey lived in Har-lem in the 1920s. It's interesting to see the constant movement of the community to which you belong.

FP Albert deeply admires Marcus Garvey. Does this historical figure in-spire you more than Sekou Touré?

MC What a comparison! Garvey never had the opportunity to wield power, so he never got his hands dirty.

FP Nonetheless, he was accused of embezzlement. . . .

MC Maybe, but he wasn't involved in oppression and corruption, whereas Sekou Touré was truly the dictator par excellence. In my opinion, Gar-vey and Sekou Touré should not be compared. They have nothing in common!

FP Don't you think Garvey's wish to return to African sources was some-what unrealistic?

MC Yes, certainly, but it is good to be unrealistic, to be utopian.

FP Was it his dream of returning to Africa that aroused your interest in him?

MC His excesses interested me. He would dress like an emperor, don a feathered helmet, and ride through the streets of Harlem in an open car-riage. Intellectuals like Du Bois hated him. This man, who had a tre-mendous impact upon the masses but was spurned by the bourgeoisie, appealed to me. He was embarrassing and stepped on people's toes. They didn't know what to do with him. He would deliver thunderous speeches and embarrass everybody, and they all wanted to get rid of him.

Even the Ku Klux Klan wanted to eliminate him. I liked his iconoclastic side.

FP *Tree of Life*'s title in French, *La vie scélérate*, which means "wretched life," is rather somber. Why did you choose it?

MC My mother would often say, "La vi sé an séléwat" and "Fout la vi séléwat." This was a way of saying that life causes you a lot of misfortunes. It is a common proverb in Guadeloupean Creole.

FP People don't expect anything from life because it is wretched? Isn't this a kind of fatalism?

MC Of course. It's the type of fatalism we mentioned earlier. My mother reflected it, although she was a very combative human being as well.

FP Who is Coco, the narrator? Is it you?

MC No, in fact, it isn't. I borrowed my eldest daughter's identity and birthdate (which appears in the first chapter of the third part of the novel), and she is the narrator. This allowed me to include myself in the story in order to criticize my own actions and those of people of my generation. Thécla, Coco's mother, spends her youth pursuing the revolution, but she ends up marrying a White man and leading a middle-class life. Coco ridicules in passing the militant literature her mother dreamed of.

FP The beginning of *Tree of Life* takes place in Panama. Then you mention very specific historical events and facts such as World War I, the number of Guadeloupean soldiers who died for France (1,673, to be precise). Why do you find it necessary to include these and other historical facts in a fictional narrative?

MC I already mentioned the interplay between history and memory. It's also in the postmodernist tradition. Historical facts authenticate a purely fictional narrative, which proceeds to subvert them, since what is essential is not history but fiction. For instance, Malcolm X's death doesn't make a difference in the novel, but that of Thécla's lover does, a man not known to history but only to personal memory.

FP There are also a lot of historical figures, Jamaicans and others. We already talked about Marcus Garvey and African-Americans. . . . Is this still part of the interplay between history and memory?

MC It also stresses a certain view of history. I want to stress that the African Diaspora in the West Indies and the Americas has a common history and shares the same heroes, dreams, and aspirations. Members of the African Diaspora should not remain isolated within their national shells. It's not a Pan Africanist ideal per se, but rather a way for diaspora members to claim a common heritage.

FP After working in Panama under rather harsh conditions, Albert goes back to Guadeloupe, where he changes. The victim becomes the victimizer. Why?

MC I would not use the term *victimizer*. Let's simply say that Albert is totally engrossed in himself and his social climbing. It's human. He is not an exemplary hero devised to teach lessons.

FP *Tree of Life* describes a color-based hierarchy. Is that type of social stratification still evident in Guadeloupe?

MC *Tree of Life* portrays the emergence of a Black middle-class family several decades ago. At that time color was not just important, it was an essential question. Think back to the pyramid at the time of slavery: Whites, mulattoes, Blacks. This is largely no longer true. The issue of color has lost much of its significance as Guadeloupean society moves toward racial harmony. However, let's not minimize the color question, because Blacks still constitute the majority of the poor.

FP In the novel, a certain number of characters improve their social condition through education. This reminds me of similar endeavors by the young José and his grandmother in the book *Black Shack Alley*. African-Americans in the United States are growing more doubtful about achieving integration through education. Do people in the West Indies still believe in the merits of education?

MC We shouldn't mix everything up. The era during which *Tree of Life* takes place is not very distant from that of Zobel's *Black Shack Alley*. For Black people at that time, education was the only means of improving social status and "leaving the cane fields behind." In those days, Blacks obeyed the famous Victor Schoelcher dictate: "Hard work will make people forget your African ancestors." Nowadays, society is shaped along class lines and is more rigid. It is more difficult to move into a higher class. In addition, there is the problem of employment. In Guadeloupe, as in France and in the United States, from what you tell me, young people wonder whether schools and universities aren't simply factories producing unemployed people.

FP What would you say about people's relationship to the supernatural, which is so important in *Tree of Life*? Is it part of magic realism? Is it irony, as in *I, Tituba, Black Witch of Salem*?

MC It's more the latter. I enjoyed myself immensely depicting the reconciliation between Liza's and Elaise's spirits as they move around old Albert. But I really don't mean to mock people's belief in spirits, which is a cultural phenomenon found in our societies. I am aware that there can be no West Indian novel without the presence of the occult, so I derisively add to it.

FP Into which languages has *Tree of Life* been translated?

MC English, Italian, and German.

FP What about *I, Tituba, Black Witch of Salem*?

MC English, Italian, German, Dutch, and Spanish.

FP And *Pays mêlé*?

MC *Pays mêlé* has been translated only into German.

FP Let's discuss *Crossing the Mangrove*. What does the title mean?

MC I am referring there to the *Robert Dictionary* definition of *mangrove* as "a plant formation commonly found on tropical shores where buttonwood and mangrove trees are intermingled."

FP It's an extremely dense, thick area that is difficult to penetrate. Is this a portrayal of life?

MC Yes, maybe. I first selected the title *Traversée de la Mangrove* because it referred to a beautiful image and had a sound soft to the ear. Its symbolic correlation came later.

FP The novel's protagonist, Francis Sancher, is portrayed as a loquacious and generous character, but he does not have much stature. He seems to be an antihero. Nevertheless, he is a true catalyst who raises people's awareness about what they have never wanted or been able to do. In a way he liberates some of the other characters. Isn't this antihero who pushes others to assert themselves a bit paradoxical?

MC I didn't perceive him that way. I saw a marginalized stranger who was rejected by everyone but two women, Mira and Vilma. After his death people realize that he was, in spite of himself, a force within the village. It may be a contradiction, but this is not what interested me.

FP What did?

MC I was interested in the character of the stranger – me, for instance, in Montebello, or Francis Sancher at Rivière au Sel – how people react to him, how they define themselves in relation to him, how he influences them, how they affect him.

FP Does Rivière au Sel represent Montebello?

MC Yes, to a certain extent, with the distortion of fiction.

FP In the book there is frequent mention of a sin committed by Francis

Sancher's ancestor that affects him. Could you elaborate on the theme of sin in *Crossing the Mangrove?*

MC Although he is not a symbolic character, I believe Francis Sancher portrays the European vis-à-vis the West Indian world. The European is responsible for slavery, the slave trade, and for all sorts of wrongdoings during the colonial period. Since he belongs to the European world, Francis Sancher is answerable for this sin. The entire history of his family is an attempt to expiate and escape from this sin-related guilt. But nobody can do this, and Francis dies the same way his father died before him. He also has two sons who will probably meet the same end.

FP In your novel everyone tells how they perceived Francis Sancher, the man from elsewhere, whose origin is a mystery.

MC In this book I mostly worked on the narrative structure and gave new thought to this matter. Instead of telling the story in a linear fashion, I decided to relate it from the viewpoints of different narrators. The reader will never exactly know who Francis Sancher is. He is like a puzzle with several pieces missing.

FP Why did you adopt this new structure?

MC Because you have to change, experiment, and go in new directions. You cannot always tell stories the same way. I narrated *Segu* from Dousika Traoré to Omar and Samuel. Then in *Tree of Life* I started to experiment with a narrator reconstructing events that occurred before her birth. However, the order remained chronological. You went from Albert to Coco. In *Crossing the Mangrove*, I wanted to experiment with a circular structure, a narrative with no true beginning or end. That's how the pattern of a wake imposed itself on me. People surround a dead person, remember him and the type of person he was, and the events of his life are pieced together little by little.

FP So, even if the other characters try to reconstruct Francis Sancher's life during the wake, they mainly become aware of who they are?

MC Yes, that's the purpose of a wake. At the wake for a deceased person, you think about your own life and future death. You shed tears over the corpse you will become tomorrow.

FP How do people conceptualize death in the French West Indies? Do they see it as a passage to another world or an end in and of itself?

MC At first, slaves viewed death as a great liberation. It enabled them to go back to Africa and regain their freedom and a state of happiness. That's why death is accompanied by a joyful wake where people drink rum and tell stories. Catholicism reinforced the notion that death is not an end but the beginning of a new life. Consequently, death is almost a happy time, a sort of liberation, but I believe that this concept has lost much of its meaning over time.

FP Don't you also have in the West Indies the African notion that death is a passage to the ancestors' world?

MC I don't believe so. It's mostly the slaves' notion of liberation grafted onto Catholic belief. But now all these beliefs are less important.

FP Wakes include dancing, singing, and storytelling. Is this kind of ritual still common in the West Indies today?

MC It has practically disappeared. People may hold wakes in rural areas but without much music, singing, or dancing. We have occasionally attended wakes in Montebello, but not much was going on.

FP In *Crossing the Mangrove* some chapters are in the first person and others in the third person. Why?

MC Some chapters came to me in the first person and others in the third. I don't quite know why. I cannot explain it rationally. Later on, I noticed that narratives by female characters were in the first person. Then I realized that this was maybe more natural for me. I must have felt more distant from characters like Loulou or Désinor the Haitian, since their chapters are in the third person. It may depend on the relationship between writers and characters during the writing. I don't believe there is any given rule.

FP The quest for mythical or biological ancestors is a theme frequently encountered in your novels. We start with Veronica, in *Heremakhonon*, looking for a "nigger with ancestors," and in *Crossing the Mangrove* we end up with Francis Sancher's son Quentin, who will seek his ancestors as well.

MC To seek one's ancestors is to search for oneself. You seek an ancestor because you want to know yourself. Any literature is a search and an expression of self that always implies the knowledge of one's ancestors. Any literature is an attempt to portray yourself, to situate yourself in the world, to define yourself in relationship to others and to yourself. People don't write for any other reason. Marcel Proust's *Remembrance of Things Past* is probably the most beautiful search for self and one's milieu that has ever existed. Since I deal with another historical era, Veronica's search is different from Proust's. If people knew themselves, they would not write. There is not one novelist for whom "I" is a given entity. You have to explain, elucidate, and journey through that "I." Whether it is written by Whites or Blacks, English or Chinese, literature is a search for self, an effort to elucidate oneself.

FP In *Crossing the Mangrove* you depict a luxuriant, tropical, natural setting. You told me people had accused you of *doudouisme* [exoticism]. Why?

MC Militant friends have accused me in interviews of practicing exoticism by devoting long passages of the book to depictions of nature. Such criticism seems unfair. Guadeloupe's nature deserves a place in literary works. It speaks, has its own voice and moods. You must remember that I wrote *Crossing the Mangrove* after being out of the country for a long time. I was wonderstruck by its nature as I rediscovered it.

FP Several literary critics, including Bernard Magnier and Michael Lucey, noticed an ambience reminiscent of Faulkner's novels in *Crossing the Mangrove*. What do you think of this comparison?

MC It may apply more to the narrative structure than the atmosphere. I have read a lot of Faulkner – as I told you, he is one of my favorite authors – and, in particular, *As I Lay Dying*, where everything is organized around Addie Bundren's corpse.

FP *Crossing the Mangrove* raises contemporary issues such as the integration problem faced by Haitian immigrants. Is this an important problem in Guadeloupe today?

MC I believe it is. There are a lot of Haitians and Dominicans in Guadeloupe, and people talk about them all the time, wondering how they will fit in with the local population. People have prejudices against Dominicans, but less so against Haitians, who are more accepted, perhaps due to certain cultural similarities. But they are poor, live in isolated villages, cut sugarcane, and do the jobs nobody else wants. Sometimes Guadeloupeans regard the darker Haitians with a certain amount of contempt.

FP In the old days the West Indians looked down on East Indians who had been brought by the French to cut sugarcane after the abolition of slavery in 1848. For a long time people pejoratively called them "coolies." Have Dominicans and Haitians replaced them at the bottom of the social ladder?

MC Maybe. Not only have East Indians been integrated, but they now wield economic power. They grow and control food crops and play an

Patrick Rameau as Ishmael and Jane White as Emma in *The Tropical Breeze Hotel* performed at the Ubu Repertory Theater, New York City, February 14–26, 1995 (photo by Jonathan Slaff).

Maryse Condé, 1958 (Maryse Condé Collection).

Maryse Condé with her children in Ghana, 1966. From left to right: Aïcha, Denis (at rear), Leïla, Sylvie (Maryse Condé Collection).

Maryse Condé and Gambian actor James Campbell at the Théâtre National de Chaillot, Paris, 1975 (Maryse Condé Collection).

Mamadou Condé, Maryse Condé's
first husband, 1981 (Maryse Condé
Collection).

Pape Oumar Diop Makenna (left) as
Oluwémi d'Ajumako and Domin-
ique Raymond Marcel Gomis as
Ange in Mort d'Oluwémi
d'Ajumako (Death of Oluwemi
from Ajumako) performed in
Dakar, Senegal, 1981 (Maryse
Condé Collection).

Maryse Condé with Nobel Prize
winner Derek Walcott (St. Lucia)
and Jean-Claude Nicolas, president
of the Caribbean anglophone
literary association, ASCODELA
(right), Guadeloupe, 1991 (Maryse
Condé Collection).

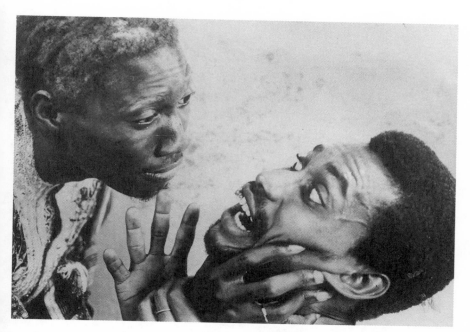

Maryse Condé and husband, Richard
Philcox, at joint reading, Chapters
Bookstore, Washington DC, 1992
(photo by Françoise Pfaff).

Maryse Condé interviewed by
Françoise Pfaff at Condé's home,
Washington DC, 1992 (photo by
Richard Philcox).

Maryse Condé lecturing at La Maison
Française, French Embassy, Wash-
ington DC, 1993 (photo by Françoise
Pfaff).

House in the middle-class Pointe-à-
Pitre neighborhood where Maryse
Condé lived as a child, 1994 (photo by
Françoise Pfaff).

important role in politics. The recent East Indian Heritage Festival showed the dynamism of their culture.

FP Have East Indians been able to preserve their culture within Guadeloupean society?

MC You have probably noticed that they have temples here, which means that they have kept some of their religious practices. The festival was held in Saint François and attracted people of East Indian origin from Réunion, Guiana, Surinam, and other areas of the world. Young people learn East Indian dances and some women wear saris. A lot of East Indians go to India on vacation. It's a somewhat mythical return to India, similar to Blacks' return to Africa.

FP In *Crossing the Mangrove* you describe a well-to-do East Indian family that seems to reflect aspects of Guadeloupean society. The book contains a certain number of illegitimate children. Does this also correspond to reality on the island?

MC It is well known that a significant portion of the children here are illegitimate. This is not a new problem.

FP Is going with several women at the same time a carryover from the African tradition of polygamy?

MC I don't think a tradition can endure for three or four centuries in a different environment with different social pressures. I believe the practice you refer to is a product of the West Indian microcosm and all that it generates.

FP When I look at your work up to *Crossing the Mangrove*, I see several directions: revolutionary plays; intimist, introspective, and highly political novels such as *Heremakhonon* and *A Season in Rihata*; sagas on the Black Diaspora in *Segu* and even *Tree of Life*; then a return to the Americas, with *I, Tituba, Black Witch of Salem*, and to a more intimist atmosphere in *Crossing the Mangrove* and, to a certain extent, in *Tree of Life*. Would you agree with this classification?

MC I think authors always write the same book, and I don't see that much difference between one book and another.

FP Are you saying there is no difference between *Heremakhonon* and *Crossing the Mangrove*?

MC If you look closely at the characters in both novels, you will find women searching for something, children who are unhappy, and men who haven't found anything. The deep themes of those books are the same, though their surface themes are different. Of course, *Here-makhonon* takes place in Africa and deals with political power, whereas *Crossing the Mangrove* is set in the West Indies. But the difficulty involved in merely living, finding a little bit of happiness, and establishing a good relationship with another person creates a problematic found in both novels. I don't see periods in my work. I think that all my books simply say the same thing in different settings.

FP In *Lettres Créoles* (Creole letters), Confiant and Chamoiseau state that you begin to question your relationship to the French language in *Crossing the Mangrove*. Is this accurate?

MC Not quite. I started to call it into question after *Tree of Life*. I had written only part of that book in Guadeloupe, whereas *Crossing the Mangrove*, as I told you before, was entirely conceived here, where people's way of speaking constantly drew my attention. It was not merely the Creole they were using, but their way of deconstructing and reconstructing the French language. I had to rethink the way I wrote in order to be faithful to the community I wanted to describe.

FP So you incorporated Creole, or rather Creolized French, into your written text. What does Creole represent for you?

MC This is very complicated. I didn't speak Creole during my childhood, even on the playground at school, where I was surrounded by children raised like me who spoke French. Then I lived abroad for years without speaking Creole to anyone. Consequently, I had barely practiced Creole. Back in Guadeloupe, Creole caught my attention even though it has always been somewhat remote from me. Although I strive to reproduce rhythms and sonorities in what I write, I don't feel any urgency to express myself in Creole. This is why a certain critic, the same one who wrote about *Heremakhonon* in *Le Naif*, . . .

FP He is pursuing you!

MC . . . said that "the mayonnaise did not set up" in *Crossing the Mangrove*. I think I don't live Creole the way other West Indians do.

FP Does this make you any less West Indian?

MC The debate on this is endless. I don't think you should make mastery of Creole the key element in West Indian identity, when you take into account the history of exile and displacement of our peoples. When I was at the University of Nanterre, I taught West Indian literature to "second-generation children," as they are commonly called. They were motivated and very eager to learn but were unable to speak Creole.

Where should they be placed? Should they be excluded from the West Indian people? In the United States some of my Haitian students no longer know French, much less Creole. Are they too to be excluded?

FP So how do you define West Indian identity?

MC As a matter of fact, I don't. It's not a recipe for cooking. People live a culture, and I believe that there are several ways of living your West Indian identity and your relationship to Creole and popular culture. I think Naipaul is as West Indian as Derek Walcott, though one flauntingly denies it and the other celebrates it.

Haïti chérie; The Hills of Massabielle
and Various Other Plays

NEW YORK CITY, NOVEMBER 13, 1991

5

FP I just read *Haïti chérie* (Beloved Haiti) on the train to New York this morning. I'd never had access to it before.

MC It's a children's book.

FP Why did you choose that title? It reminds me of the name of a Haitian song and seems almost ironic.

MC I didn't choose the title. I wanted to call it *Lan mizé pa dou*, which is a West Indian proverb meaning "It's no fun to be poor" or "Misery's not sweet." But the people at Bayard Press rejected the Creole title and chose *Haïti chérie* instead.

FP If people associate your narrative with the song "Haïti chérie," they might envision Haiti as something to be cherished, whereas the country has its portion of misery.

MC The song also says that there is no country more beautiful or sweeter than Haiti. But if you are aware that there are thousands of Haitian refugees and boat people all around, you realize that this sweet country is in fact quite bitter. The same image is contained in Maurice Lemoine's *Sucre amer* (Bitter sugar). In works by the Cuban poet Nicolás Guillén, you also find a type of sugar that doesn't sweeten. This is the reality of the West Indies. These are countries that appear to be attractive and pleasant but that are actually very hard.

FP The title, then, is not meant to be ironic?

MC The publishing house people who selected the title are not stupid, and they did put a certain irony into it.

FP *Haïti chérie* tells the story of Rose-Aimée, a thirteen-year-old Haitian girl who leaves her village to look for work in the city. As she experiences injustices and mistreatment, she begins to dream of going to Miami. Rose-Aimée eventually drowns along with other boat people off the shores of the United States. Did you write this book for your granddaughter Raki?

MC No, Bayard asked me for a children's story for its *Je bouquine* collection. Since I am not interested in spinning tales, I replied that I would tell a highly contemporary story. They raised their eyebrows and explained to me that very contemporary stories could not be told to children of eleven or twelve. When I gave them the manuscript, they didn't object to it, though they still thought it was not really a children's story.

FP I had the same feeling.

MC Originally, they wanted to change the ending. But the story, published in 1988 in *Je bouquine* magazine, turned out to be so popular that the children themselves requested its publication as a book.

FP What kind of magazine is *Je bouquine*?

MC A children's magazine with full-length stories and comic strips. "Haïti chérie" was published as a story, and the children loved it. They were discovering Haiti, injustice, racism, the boat people, and such. Children are much more intelligent than people generally think. I have in my possession some five hundred letters from children about the story. They also sent so many letters to *Je bouquine* that the editors decided to publish the story as a book, which appeared in 1991. The children's reaction means that you can tell them anything, so long as you don't talk over their heads. They raised a lot of questions, and some of them asked me why I hadn't chosen a different ending and allowed Rose-Aimée to build a house in New York for her mother. I told them that I could not end the story differently because it was based on facts. They understood this quite well. It was my first children's book, and my experience with it was quite moving.

FP In *Haïti chérie* you have a lot to say about dignity and rebellion. Each time there is an injustice, Rose-Aimée and her friends rebel. There is even a girl who steals money from her abusive employer – theft as a response to injustice. Might some sections of the book influence children in a negative way?

MC When people are mistreated, they react in all sorts of ways. *Haïti chérie* is not a book about morals. It tells a story as it presented itself. Yes, it so happens that in an unjust situation, people respond to injustice with injustice. I am not saying that this is particularly good, but it does happen. The story is not meant to be exemplary.

FP It does teach children about Haiti's history and social conditions.

MC I remember questioning children before writing the story. I asked kids in my neighborhood in Paris whether they knew anything about Haiti, and they said they didn't. So I decided to draw their attention to this country. Later, when I settled in Guadeloupe, I found that a lot of Haitian children felt marginalized in schools there. When I talked about this book to schoolchildren, the Haitian kids were very happy to find a story located in their country. This made me realize that *Haïti chérie* had touched a sensitive spot.

FP Were these children regaining their Haitian heritage?

MC They were happy. Some were also very intimidated and would hate to see me come to their class because they knew we were going to talk about Haiti and draw attention to them. Children are very complex, and they don't want to be noticed as different. This story would usually hurt a few of them. You had to be clever to get them to talk.

FP You describe Haiti as a very poor country, and I can easily understand why some children would hesitate to admit a connection to it.

MC This would again stress their status as marginalized, immigrant children who came from a problem-ridden country. Often the teacher would tell me that there were Haitian children in the class, but they didn't want to be identified as such. However, some of them would finally raise their hands and want to talk after a period of discussion. Their reaction was not always immediate.

FP So *Haïti chérie* had the merit of provoking a certain amount of discussion?

MC Yes, it circulated widely in schools and was very successful as a children's book. French kids would write me and say, "I didn't know children my age could work. I didn't know that ten- or twelve-year-old children could work and be separated from their parents." They were deeply moved.

FP This also allowed them to discover Haiti's class system.

MC What impressed them was the extreme poverty. It hurt them that you could leave your father and mother to go to the city, and that you could work in a lady's house and be insulted, poorly paid, and even beaten. In general, they accepted the heroine's death, especially since it was not described directly.

FP Indeed, the people on the boat are engulfed by the sea. You write, "They all slipped into the other world. Death is not an end. It opens onto a world of beyond where there are no poor and rich, no uneducated and educated people, no Blacks, Mulattoes and Whites . . ." (83). Death is not an end but rather the transition toward an egalitarian afterworld. This calls to mind the Senegalese writer Birago Diop, for whom "the dead are not dead," an African concept also found in Haiti. At this point and elsewhere in the story, you explain Haiti and its traditions. It is important to provide this type of knowledge and open kids up to other cultures through reading.

MC As I told you, it was the poverty in the story that interested them. In fact, when you read Bettelheim's books, you realize that children are traumatized by death, separation from their parents, poverty, and child labor. Children didn't consider the somewhat exotic aspect of my book. They identified with Rose-Aimée and actually cried.

FP Right now, you are in New York City for the performance of your play *The Hills of Massabielle* ("Le morne de Massabielle"), written in 1972 but as yet unpublished in French. The English version was presented last night at the Ubu Repertory Theater. You wrote this play around the same time as *Dieu nous l'a donné*, didn't you? Has it been staged before?

MC Actually, it was written before *Dieu nous l'a donné* and was the first long work I wrote. It was performed in Puteaux in 1979 before a group of friends, and we had a lot of fun. The director back then was Gabriel García, an Argentine who staged the play in a very particular way, with two actors, one Black and one White, to play the role of Jean-Marie, who is a mulatto. The Black performed with the White in his shadow. García invented a set with a whole series of small rectangles in which the action took place. It looked like the facade of a New York City skyscraper lit up at night; sometimes one rectangle was lit, sometimes another. It was a bit surrealistic, which was fashionable then. Last night the play was performed in a realistic way and staged differently. I was pleasantly surprised to see it interpreted in another way. The play was written more than twenty years ago, and if I didn't publish it, it's because I didn't really like it and was not too interested in having it published. I considered it a play written early in my career, but I must admit that I rediscovered it with pleasure yesterday evening. I laughed a lot again.

FP Last night the play was staged and performed by African-Americans and West Indians. Did this significantly change its representation?

MC At Puteaux the actors were also Black, except for the one White I mentioned who played Jean-Marie along with a Black actor. Sidiki Bakaba performed as Jean-Marie, Bienvenue Neba was Sylvain, and Lydia Ewandé played Judith. They were all good actors, and it was quite different. Yesterday the play was performed somewhat like a comedy, whereas the first time it was presented in a more serious manner.

FP How did the press receive the play originally?

MC There was no press. Not a line was written about it in the papers.

FP Who provided the money to stage it?

MC The Hauts de Seine Theater in Puteaux, a very beautiful Italian-style building. The theater director himself paid the actors. The play was also performed at the American Cultural Center in a smaller theater, similar to the one here in New York City.

FP Do you think the New York public reacted favorably to the play? Do you feel the message of the play can be understood and appreciated by 1991 audiences?

MC There aren't that many messages in the play. It's a comedy about the arrival of tourists and life in a small community, with rebels as well as nonrebels who want to profit from the manna of tourism. It's a rather lighthearted comedy, and it seemed to me last night that the audience appreciated it. Of course, in 1979 the performance was in French, and you always prefer your text in the language in which you wrote it. A written text is always more beautiful and poetic in its original language. It may happen that images and subtleties are not conveyed in a translation and may well be untranslatable. A play should be adapted, almost rewritten, instead of simply translated.

FP Could you give examples from your play that are so essentially Guadeloupean that they might be untranslatable?

MC In Guadeloupean and Martinican Creole, a *béké* is a White person born in the West Indies. Using the Jamaican equivalent, *bakra*, doesn't make sense for an American audience, which won't know what the term means. I think you should keep the original word, *béké*, when the translation won't be any better understood. We could say the same about words like *bami* and *doukounou*, the names of Jamaican pastries and dishes used in this English version of the play. We should be able to find a way to signify such terms within the play's context. I am not sure it is useful to render them with equivalent words from an Anglophone West Indian context.

FP You mentioned to me that you would change certain scenes if you rewrote the play today. Which ones?

MC For instance, the wake scene after Leandre's death is not polished enough. Either it was not needed or was insufficiently developed. Now, twenty years later, I would cut the wake or make the scene longer, with dances and songs to create an interlude, a sort of popular theater reviving local folklore. I didn't like the ending either. I found it somewhat confusing, but perhaps that was due to the performance by the actor playing the part of the old man. I thought it was not up to par. You shouldn't ask a young man of thirty to make himself up as an old man and then stutter and sputter. The ending, which was already not too good in terms of the script, was not improved by this unconvincing character.

FP Was your play originally written for a French or a West Indian audience?

MC I wrote the play for both audiences, since it is hard to dissociate a West Indian audience from a French one. Both are quite enmeshed. Since *The Hills of Massabielle* doesn't have a lot of Creolisms, a French audience has no problems understanding.

FP How did people in New York come to stage the play?

MC I don't know how. Françoise Kourilsky, director of the Ubu Repertory Theater, called me and proposed it. Since it was a play I had completely forgotten, I recommended *The Tropical Breeze Hotel* (*Pension Les Alizés*) instead. Yet she didn't want to stage *The Tropical Breeze Hotel* because it has only two characters, like the Ina Césaire play that she was presenting at the same minifestival. She wanted a play with lots of characters that would be different from Ina's, so she preferred *The Hills of Massabielle*.

FP You wrote three theater works at the beginning of your literary career. Are you now less tempted by the theater?

MC I still write plays. In 1988 I wrote *The Tropical Breeze Hotel*, which has been performed in Guadeloupe and Martinique. Another play, *An Tan Revolisyon: Elle court, elle court la liberté* (Revolution time: The elusiveness of freedom), deals with the abolition of slavery in Guadeloupe. It was commissioned, published, and staged by the Regional Council of Guadeloupe in 1989 for the bicentenary of the French Revolution.

FP What is the theme of *The Tropical Breeze Hotel*?

MC The play portrays the encounter in Paris between a Guadeloupean cabaret dancer and a Haitian physician who is a political refugee. They dream of going to Haiti to open a small hotel they will name the Tropical Breeze Hotel, where they can rebuild their lives. The political refugee later abandons the dancer, and she ends up alone, quite unhappy and disappointed.

FP What inspired the plot for this play?

MC It's a play I wrote for Sonia Emmanuel, who is both an actress and a dear friend of mine. I noticed that she couldn't find good roles in Paris, which is generally the case for Black actors in France. I wanted to write a play for her so she could display her talents. She had successfully presented *The Hills of Massabielle* in Guadeloupe but was never able to stage it in Paris. She wanted to have it performed at cultural centers or the Avignon Theater Festival, but this never happened. In the end, I think she also felt a bit frustrated.

FP Did Sonia Emmanuel influence you in terms of the play's text and style?

MC I wanted to provide her with a text that suited her nature as an actress. She is somewhat intense but is also a rather controlled person. Deep inside her, there is a lot of tenderness and even nostalgia. I wrote the play knowing she would be able to get into the Emma character.

FP Where did you get Emma, this rather pathetic character who is a former cabaret dancer?

MC She reflects the rise and fall of a person. She is the old prostitute, the aging whore. These are themes found frequently in the theater.

FP In this play we recognize feelings of resignation and fatalism present in some of your other works. Ismael, the Haitian physician, repeating the words of his former Haitian mistress, says, "There is no happiness for Blacks." Is this the expression of malediction again?

MC Coming from a doctor, a man of good social and educational status, you cannot call it malediction. But our history is not a combative one, and many people believe that a sort of fatality burdens us and prevents us from fulfilling ourselves. For Ismael, these are moments of despair.

Actually, he is involved in an activist political movement and returns to Haiti to try to participate in a political struggle. Therefore, I believe that his actions contradict the fatalistic aspect of his personality.

FP   Still, he is very disappointed. He comes from the elite and wants to join the peasant struggle. Don't these individuals who want to abandon their own class to espouse the cause of a different class actually fight a battle that is lost from the start?

MC   Everybody from Fidel Castro to Jacques Stéphen Alexis does this. The intellectual always wishes to join the masses and participate in their struggle. It's a constant in Caribbean thought.

FP   In *The Tropical Breeze Hotel* Ismael barks at Emma concerning Haiti, "You know nothing! Nothing at all! No one knows anything. There's no one truth . . ." [Brewster Lewis and Temerson translation, 131]. Is this a philosophical attitude that matches your own?

MC   Everyone recognizes that there is no truth, since everybody tells his or her own truth and offers his or her own point of view of a given situation. In the end, people are unable to know what is true, accurate, or false.

FP   This play starts and ends with a soliloquy. At both the beginning and the end, Emma is alone on stage. She wears the same clothes, although they are dirty at the end. During the first scene, she reminisces about the time when she was a nude dancer, saying, "When I'd stick on my false eyelashes, that's when the show would begin" [119]. At the end, she says something similar: "I'll stick on my false eyelashes, and the show can begin!" [164]. Is this a comment about the masks people wear in life? For you, does this cyclical structure reflect the search for a new dramatic form?

MC   I once wanted to write a play about Lisette Malidor. I was attracted by her and her experiences, but the play was never written because she didn't confide enough in me. The words you quote are hers. She herself would say, "When I put on my false eyelashes, the show would begin!" This impressed me because I could see at that very moment that she went from one world to another. She was switching from real life to the stage, a world where she was the queen. Everyone gravitated to her, the central figure. Her words came back to me while I was imagining the character of a dethroned actress who had known moments of grandeur. To bring a two-character play like this to an end, it is tempting to have the same monologue at the beginning and end to show that things have come full circle and that there is no exit. You cannot say that Emma goes in another direction at the end of the play. She is a bit more distressed than she was at the beginning, but in the final analysis nothing has really changed.

FP *The Tropical Breeze Hotel* was performed in Guadeloupe and in Martinique. How did West Indian audiences react to it?

MC I was not in Guadeloupe at the time, although based on what I know, the theater was packed and audiences there liked the play. But after it opened, I was violently attacked by a communist woman because I said that Pointe-à-Pitre had turned into nothing but a bunch of concrete buildings. She perceived this as an attack on the communist city government and apparently decided to calm her nerves by writing an open letter to the newspaper. Such is the level of criticism in Guadeloupe! I have no further comment on this.

FP Let's look at *An Tan Revolisyon: Elle court, elle court la liberté*. Is this play written in Creole, as its title would seem to indicate?

MC Parts of the play are in Creole, but it's mostly in French. Based on the French text, actors have to improvise in Creole.

FP What are the themes and characters in this play?

MC The slaves, the arrival of Victor Hughes, the restoration of slavery, the issue of the Haitian revolution that people tried unsuccessfully to spread to Guadeloupe, the ties between Guadeloupean slaves and Haitian Blacks, the relationship to Bonaparte, and the like. It's a spectacular production, a large-scale epic fresco, which I intended as a popular drama with music, songs, and sixty characters, counting extras. In Guadeloupe it was performed at the Fleur d'Epée Fort and was well received by mass audiences.

FP I understand you had a hand in the mise-en-scène of the play. What was your role?

MC I suggested three performance areas to represent the West Indies, France, and Haiti, in other words, a series of stages on which the play would be performed. The play was presented outdoors, and director Sonia Emmanuel selected three sections of the open-air theater to represent the various sites where the action took place.

FP Isn't it slightly problematic when the playwright deals with the mise-en-scène? Doesn't it limit the freedom of the actors and the director?

MC No, Sonia did what she wanted. In order to imagine the play, I had to conceive its staging. It was not a traditional drama built on dialogue. We needed collective scenes, dances, encounters, different spaces. I had to envision the play's staging in my head, but I did not provide directions, only suggestions.

FP This kind of performance must have required a lot of work and money.

MC The Regional Council provided us with a subsidy of 700,000 francs, which is a rather significant amount of money in Guadeloupe.

FP Do you have other plays in mind?

MC In 1989 I wrote "Comédie d'amour" (Comedy of love), for José Jernidier, who will stage it for the first time in April 1993.

FP What can you say about it?

MC It's the story of two sisters, one of whom doesn't work outside the home. In addition, she might to a certain extent represent the stereotype of the West Indian woman.

FP Does it take place in a bourgeois setting?

MC No, it's a low-income family. The woman doesn't work, her husband is a deliveryman, and she has two children in school. She takes in her sister, who has just lost her husband and who used to belong to a higher social class. Her husband had been a schoolteacher, and they owned a nice house, as befits the family of a low-level civil servant. So the widow comes to live with her sister and her husband and two children. She stays for a long time because she can't console herself about her husband's death. After two years, considerable tension has developed between the two sisters and among the rest of the family. The tension builds and suddenly erupts, causing scenes when the characters tell each other a few homegrown truths. Nevertheless, the play is a comedy. One of the couple's children does everything possible to reconcile her mother and her aunt. "All's well that ends well." "Comédie d'amour" is a play about the life of a family. Should people say what they really think to others? Can people love one another and still tell the truth? Or should they hide the truth from those they love? The play shows tensions between sisters, and *The Hills of Massabielle* has similar sibling tensions in the confrontation between Luana and Judith. I realized during the performance last night that this theme was already of interest to me when I wrote *The Hills of Massabielle*: two sisters love each other but also envy each other. One believes she has succeeded in life while the other has failed. But where is the final truth? Who succeeded and who failed? It's impossible to know.

MC I recently discovered that you wrote a play in 1986 called "Les sept voyages de Ti-Noël" (Ti-Noel's seven voyages). What is it about, and why haven't you published it?

FP It's a play I wrote in collaboration with José Jernidier for his theater troupe, Plus Bakanal, to commemorate the anniversary of the abolition of slavery. It depicts the migrations of the West Indian people from the beginning of their history to the present: the slave trade, movement to Panama, migration to France through the BUMIDOM [government agency created to facilitate movement to France by West Indian workers], and so forth. The play was devised for a specific occasion and only half was in written form. There was a script from which the actors improvised.

FP Who is the Ti-Noël character?

MC He represents West Indian man from the time he was a slave up to today.

FP The plays we have just discussed indicate that the theater still interests you. Ten years ago you said you were no longer writing plays because considerable financial resources were required to stage them. Have you changed your mind?

MC No, because I think that while I was saying that to you, I was still slightly involved with the theater. It's a medium with which I have always more or less flirted, but never with much satisfaction.

FP I have heard that someone wants to stage Segu. Is this true?

MC An African-American couple from Louisiana wants to stage Segu in the same manner as the Mahabharata. Segu would be performed over a period of five days.

The Political Arena, *Les derniers rois mages,* and More Short Stories

WASHINGTON DC, NOVEMBER 6, 1992

6

FP You just ran as a candidate in regional elections in Guadeloupe and were not elected. Last year you said that a writer should not get involved in politics. Over the course of our previous interviews, you have stated that your writings should not be perceived as militant didacticism. Have you changed your mind about political involvement? How do you reconcile the social criticism in your literature with your categorical refusal to tell others what to think? Is there a contradiction here?

MC I have never in my life written a political tract. But there are always errors in interpreting my writings because people think I have done so. They always look for militant or positive heroes, and I never portray any. Maryse Condé the individual, the citizen, is quite free to run for public office. I have said that if Guadeloupe were independent, I would certainly not occupy a position of power. But Guadeloupe is not independent and is not about to become so. And since the pro-independence party, to which I am close, won only two seats on the Regional Council, obviously we are not in the process of subverting the French state. Perhaps this is a time for us to try to assert ourselves as an opposition force. I wanted to lend a hand to friends who might need it. It wasn't very successful and in the final analysis, I didn't really help much. Things are over as far as I am concerned. I should perhaps say that I had the feeling, as did another intellectual who is also a Creolophone writer, that we were more used than truly useful: we seemed to be simply names put on a slate to try to attract a certain number of people. However, we felt that our ideas and the message we wanted to send were not heard or even mentioned during the political campaign. It was, we could say, an effort for naught.

FP How many candidates did the pro-independence people have?

MC We had a slate of forty-one candidates, of which two were elected. Of course, people will say that some parties didn't have any candidates elected at all. This is true, but some parties got seventeen or twenty. I thought our party would have at least five.

FP We should also stress that you seemingly entered the political arena without great enthusiasm. Last spring you stated, "People encouraged me to become actively involved in politics but I really didn't want to" [*Le Griot des Antilles* 17 (April–May 1992)].

MC After the enthusiasm of my twenties, I no longer sought active political involvement, because most of the time this means self-censorship. There are things you say that you don't really believe but that correspond to a sort of propaganda or mass pedagogy. During the 1968 demonstrations and strikes in France, Jean-Paul Sartre said, "Workers at the Billancourt Renault car factory should not be made to cry." My own feeling would be that if the Billancourt workers want to cry, well, let them! I do not at all enjoy active involvement, but people like to use my name, and I often allow myself to get caught up in the game.

FP What can the role of a writer be within a political party? For instance, what would your program have been had you been elected?

MC I really didn't want to get elected. I even wanted mine to be the last name on the slate, but this couldn't be, for various reasons. A writer doesn't have a political program. If writers come out with programs, they are politicians, not writers.

FP So you lent your name to the party but never thought you would be elected?

MC Precisely, and my political friends knew this; it was clear.

FP Could just being a member of a political party limit a writer's creativity and freedom of expression?

MC As far as I am concerned, it doesn't. These are two entirely different matters. The energy you have to exert to seek political office, to go to meetings, to address crowds, I prefer to dedicate to writing.

FP What was the electoral campaign like?

MC The campaign stayed at a rather high level. A few things went overboard, but overall there were no low blows, and the campaign was a good one.

FP Is an independent Guadeloupe viable in this time of large geopolitical blocs such as Europe after 1992?

MC I am not an economist and will not jump into this sort of debate. But I believe that if Dominica succeeds in becoming independent, even with some difficulty, Guadeloupe should also succeed, if everyone works for it.

FP In 1982 I asked you whether you thought the attitude of France toward the French West Indies had changed after Mitterrand took power. At the time you replied that since he had just been elected, it was too early to answer the question. With the distance of time, would you now have a response?

MC Yves Bénot, the noted French political scientist, once said, "Whether it is ruled by the Left or the Right, the metropolis is still the metropolis." I believe this is an answer.

FP And a very good one at that! Now, if you agree, let's talk about your 1992 novel, *Les derniers rois mages* (The last Magi),[2] in which you use as an epigraph the words of a Lena Horne song from the film *Stormy Weather*:

> Don't know why
> there's no sun up in the sky
> Stormy weather
> since my man and I ain't together
> It's raining all the time

Why did you choose these words? Do you particularly like Lena Horne, or did you want to announce the presence of the African-American Diaspora in this work?

MC I believe the whole book is centered on one couple's problem. Men and women who live in the United States know that the major problem faced by the African-American community is the relationship between male and female. From Toni Morrison through Paule Marshall to Alice Walker, African-American novelists have spoken abundantly about it. I

2. Literally, "The last Magi." Richard Philcox's forthcoming translation is tentatively titled "The Last of the African Kings."

would even say that it has become commonplace. In the book, I too have given my viewpoint on this very common situation.

FP The African ancestor of your last Magus closely resembles Béhanzin, king of Dahomey, who was exiled by the French and who inspired you. I knew Béhanzin had been exiled to Algeria, but I didn't know about his forced stay in Martinique. Do both these exiles match historical reality?

MC Absolutely! King Béhanzin stayed in Martinique for five years and left the island because he seemingly couldn't stand the climate, the noises, the hurricanes, and so forth. The French government showed a certain clemency toward him and instead of leaving him to die in Martinique, they sent him to Algeria.

FP How did you get interested in this story?

MC It wasn't really on my mind, but every time I went to Martinique, someone would mention it to me. The story is present in the consciousness of Martinicans. In fact, I believe there's a Martinican currently shooting a film about King Béhanzin. So someone would always remind me of King Béhanzin's captivity and show me the house in Bellevue where he had lived. People also spoke to me about his son Ouanilo, who returned to Africa and is now dead. That is how the story imposed itself on me.

FP When was Béhanzin in Martinique?

MC From 1895 to 1900.

FP Since you were not able to find eyewitnesses, was the story of Béhanzin in Martinique transmitted to you orally?

MC This is what's so striking. A man I know well, whose name I will not disclose, told me, "I went to school with Béhanzin's son." I was quite amused, because I had the dates in front of me. I knew that Béhanzin and his son went back to Africa in 1900 and that this man was about sixty-five years old. It was absolutely impossible for any encounters to have taken place, but he was convinced that they had. He even described the boy's haircut to me. When I told him it was impossible, finally he had to agree. Béhanzin is still present in the consciousness of Martinicans.

FP Why did you decide to slightly alter the course of history by having the King of Dahomey procreate in Martinique and by giving him West Indian descendants?

MC That's fiction. The story seemed rather beautiful to me, of this king who goes to Martinique, cannot live there, and leaves. I can't explain how the idea came to me. I also found this story interesting as a symbol of the relationship that West Indians always have with Africa. We always think we come from Africa. Well, we do come from Africa, but the fact that this king abandoned Martinique without leaving anything behind symbolized the relationship West Indians have with Africa. Actually, though, I didn't even think that far. I saw a very beautiful story, and my imagination worked all around it.

FP Readers will notice that the name Magus is sarcastically given at a bar to Djéré, Béhanzin's first Martinican descendant, thus the title of your book, *Les derniers rois mages*. Does the title have other symbolic meaning? It obviously recalls the manger scene and the adoration by the Three Kings. Is all of this totally ironic?

MC In the West Indies, if you want to speak about somebody who has a royal ancestor, the first and perhaps only point of comparison that comes to mind is the Magi.

FP How long did it take you to write this book?

MC About two and a half years.

FP You develop a genealogy in this work, as in many of your stories. It also depicts the decline of a lineage, a theme that you explored in *Segu*. How would you sum up the major themes in *Les derniers rois mages*?

MC First, the African–West Indian relationship, which is a difficult one. In a modest way this book may also invite African-American women to undergo a sort of self-criticism. Based only on the ones I know, of course, I wonder if they don't expect too much from a man. Don't they perhaps ask too much from him in wanting him to be a god or a king, for example? Don't they simply end up scaring him? Shouldn't they be more tolerant and humble in their relationships with men? When I talk with women friends and hear their terribly severe judgments about African-American men, I wonder whether a little more love and tenderness is needed in those interactions. Maybe then the couple could reenergize the relationship.

FP There is also the myth of the strong Black woman. Could it be that she castrates the man? Does Spéro somewhat symbolize this sort of man adrift?

MC I didn't perceive Spéro as a man adrift. I saw him simply as a man who refuses to be cast in a mold that doesn't fit him. He is an artist, somewhat a dreamer, perhaps a bit lethargic. He may not be very brave, but he accepts what can be termed his weakness. I think one must accept and like him the way he is, and see that it is very possible to have a fruitful relationship with him. But if you want to turn him into a militant who paints grand pictures of Malcolm X or Martin Luther King, if you want to make him what he is not, then you inevitably cause a disaster. This is somewhat the meaning of the book.

FP You say that he is not adrift and that he refuses to conform to a mold, yet at the end of the book he has a deep sense of failure. He almost wants to commit suicide.

MC Because his wife doesn't like him. Neither his wife nor his daughter accepts him the way he is. They both want him to be a superman. Since he cannot be a superman in their eyes, he feels a sense of failure. If they had perceived him in a different light, taking into account the love and tenderness he could bring them, he would not be so confused.

FP His confusion is translated through oneiric hallucinations in which he is attacked by crabs. What do those dreams mean?

MC All this comes from a film I saw on television. In a region of South Carolina, crabs emerge from the earth during a particular season. This had a lasting impression on me, and it reappeared in the book I was writing. But it has no symbolic import.

FP Had you ever been to the swampy areas of South Carolina where a part of your novel takes place?

MC In fact, when I lived in Virginia Richard and I went to North and South Carolina, and I was struck by the desolation of certain areas. We went to the islands where the African-American filmmaker Julie Dash shot *Daughters of the Dust*. The landscape is quite beautiful but it's also very sad, even sinister. It gives you a feeling of death. I don't know why I wanted to set my story on this small island, which is perhaps a symbol of Guadeloupe, likewise an island that doesn't always make you jump for joy.

FP Have you gone to these islands often? Have you spent a lot of time there?

MC We went several times.

FP Did you take mental notes?

MC Yes. I looked around and then worked with a map of the region in order to be precise about the various areas.

FP In an interview with Marie-Clotilde Jacquey a few years ago [*Notre Librairie*, July–September 1986], you explained that you had given more importance to men than women in *Segu* because, in fact, "in Africa men are in the foreground, they are the ones claiming that they make history." You added at the time, "If I told the story of a West Indian family, women would be in the foreground" [58]. Afterward, you wrote *Tree of Life, Crossing the Mangrove*, and *Les derniers rois mages*, which take place partially in the West Indies, yet their protagonists are still men. Why?

MC Critics often ask you questions that you are unable to answer. Marie-Clotilde Jacquey was cornering me by asking, "Why are there no women?" I responded that it was impossible to control inspiration. I cannot say to myself, "Okay, now I'm going to write a novel about women." No; this type of inspiration has to come to you, and it hasn't come to me yet. But I have written books such as *Heremakhonon* and *I, Tituba, Black Witch of Salem*, whose main characters are women.

FP Yes, but your novels about the West Indies have no female dynasties, even though matrilinear families are common in Guadeloupe and Martinique. Why is that?

MC I have not yet had the desire to do so.

FP One of the themes of your book *Les derniers rois mages* is the decline of a family and the search for an ancestor. Is this, by extension, a Black community, that of the West Indies, searching for its identity? If so, the topic appears really quite frequently in your books.

MC The quest is over. I believe that Spéro says at one point that you shouldn't live with the past, but rather put it to death, otherwise it will kill you. He understands that people must live in the present and confront present-day problems instead of constantly living with their eyes turned toward what went before, toward a more or less mythic time in the past. Spéro invites his brothers and sisters to live in the present and to fight for current issues.

FP And not for chimeras of the past?

MC That doesn't serve any purpose and only makes you very unhappy.

FP But all the same, isn't it necessary to be aware of one's past?

MC Of course you have to know your past, but you also have to integrate it into your present.

FP Your protagonist's name is Spéro, which means "I hope" in Latin. Is this name ironic?

MC Yes, obviously, but I also used to know someone named Spéro who left me with vivid memories. Such things are always personal. One

should never assume that people think through symbols. I knew someone named Spéro who was always on the verge of lassitude. He came
back to me to create my character.

FP In *Les derniers rois mages*, one of the high points of your ironic imagination is the description of the African ancestor's journey into the
world of the beyond [289–95] and his reincarnation as the son of Abebi,
a royal princess married to a brutish soldier. How did you conceive this
section of the book?

MC In Africa, people generally believe in some sort of reincarnation. As
is always the case in my work, the book contains a rather ironic and par-
odic section. So it was quite tempting to imagine the ancestor reincar-
nated in his own country at a time when things had completely changed,
when there was no longer a traditional power structure but simply military power. You cannot but wonder how he will live his new existence.

FP Spéro has an affair with a White woman, which causes a rather violent
reaction from his wife Debbie, who later bars him from her bed, although she had seemed ready to forget her husband's Black mistresses.
Are you once again denouncing the intolerance of African-Americans
toward racially mixed couples?

MC It also happened that I had just seen Spike Lee's film *Jungle Fever*, in
which the Black wife readily accepted that her husband had mistresses,
but she couldn't tolerate an Italian mistress. Having a White mistress
was the biggest crime of all. This brought grist to my mill. It can't be
said that I invented it, since Spike Lee himself talked about this extreme
intolerance. In my opinion, whether your husband cheats on you with a
White woman or a Black woman, it's the same. What's important is the
cheating.

FP People think that having a White mistress amounts to crossing over to
the enemy.

MC Yes, but since I am unable to conceive of love and sex in terms of political camps, it's a bit hard for me to agree with this concept.

FP In *Les derniers rois mages* the sections written by the king's Martinican son – "Cahiers de Djéré" (Djéré's notebooks) – take us to the myth
of the origin of the royal family and celebrate the values of African traditions. Why did you intersperse your narrative with tales? Are you becoming a griot?

MC It was mainly a concern at the level of writing, an intention to write
in a different way. The writing of tales, the writing of these particular

Djéré stories, is quite different from the writing of a novel. It was an attempt to integrate several writing styles into a text, and also an attempt to dismantle, to crumble and break up the narrative structure. You must change your way of writing; otherwise you always write the same story in the same way, which is very boring for you and the readers.

FP So this was an experiment in writing?

MC It was an experiment both in writing and in structure. It's also true that the Abomey myth of origins is quite beautiful. I had wanted to put it into a narrative for a long time. When I was writing *Segu*, I wanted to but it wasn't possible.

FP Do these tales really exist in the African oral tradition? You didn't modify them?

MC I modified them in the sense of writing them down, but they reflect the myth of the origins of the Abomey royal family.

FP In *Les derniers rois mages*, as in *Heremakhonon* and *Segu*, the reader shifts in time and space. Why did you come back to using this structure?

MC Haven't there always been shifts in what I write?

FP Yes, more or less. There are shifts in *Tree of Life*, and even more in *Heremakhonon*, to the point that readers sometimes wonder which spatial and temporal environment they are in. You seem to use this technique again in *Les derniers rois mages*. Is it because the technique suits the story, or is it your intent to make the reader participate and reconstruct the narrative, as happens with the nouveau roman?

MC This technique corresponds to the story, and I think it's also a way to get the reader involved. Instead of being passive, the reader must intervene to reconstitute the story and take an active part in the reading process, raising questions pertaining to the story and the characters. This way, the reader gets more closely involved.

FP In *Les derniers rois mages* the narrator states, "African king or not, Djéré's daddy had behaved like all the other Black men in the world. He had not taken care of his child" [18]. Won't this type of biting raillery create enemies for you, like *Heremakhonon* when it was published?

MC I believe it is commonplace to say that these fathers tend to abandon or neglect their children. In our societies, illegitimacy is routine. What I say there is not iconoclastic at all.

FP And then you add, "African, American or West Indian, the Black man is not carved from the wood of monogamists" [41]. Do you think these abrasive statements will be appreciated by Black readers?

MC In the book it is not I who speak, but rather the narrator or the characters.

FP Yes, but why do your narrators or your characters so often repeat this type of sentence?

MC In the final analysis, this corresponds to a reality. This type of paternal abdication is a recognized sociological fact.

FP Is it going to continue, or will it cease as societies become better integrated?

MC Maybe this sociological trait will vanish when people have more responsibilities within their own society. As long as people feel they don't have an impact on their future, they will always be able to escape through alcohol, drugs, and sex, and they will not assume their reponsibilities.

FP Do you believe, then, that all of this also depends on individuals' access to power within their societies?

MC I believe that people who don't have any impact on their society tend to become more and more irresponsible. But as soon as they are given the power to restructure their society, they change and are capable of doing things they hadn't even thought about doing before.

FP Do you know any examples of societies that were restructured and mentalities that were changed?

MC You need only to talk to people who work in ghettos or in underprivileged neighborhoods. They say that you just have to give responsibilities to adolescents and their behavior changes right away. This is what social work is all about. Make people responsible so that they can gradually take their lives in their own hands.

FP In *Les derniers rois mages* you also talk about women who load coal into the holds of ships [136]. Did they actually exist?

MC All that is based on history.

FP In *Les derniers rois mages* you include a significant number of cultural and historical markers linked to the past and present of the African-American community. How will the names Jacob Lawrence, Frederick Douglass, and Romare Bearden be received by Francophone readers who don't know them? Will they understand the symbolic and historical aspects of these characters? Won't these names hamper a thorough comprehension of the written text?

MC I didn't think about this, but I have always adhered to what Vèvè Clark calls her concern for "diaspora literacy." I believe that we, the people of the Black Diaspora, should know and recognize certain names. We should not have to ask who they are. Of course they can be unfamiliar to a French reader, but in an ideal situation I would hope that a West Indian reader would recognize Jacob Lawrence or Romare Bearden as painters.

FP You also mention Richard Wright, Langston Hughes, and Paul Robeson, among others.

MC It's the same principle. You could refer to Vèvè Clark's article published in *Out of the Kumbla*.

FP Should these points of reference be used, then, with didactic intent? To educate people in terms of "diaspora literacy"?

MC I think we don't know ourselves well enough. Someone just called me from Guadeloupe to tell me that a quick survey had been made, asking people, "Do you know the name Derek Walcott?" This question was asked when he received the Nobel Prize. Three out of four people had never heard the name and did not know who he was. I think that if we are more aware of our heritage and of everything we can share, exchange, and say, we will be stronger in the sort of cultural struggle in which we have been losers so far. Yesterday evening at Chapters Bookstore, a young man was surprised that I had spoken of Malcolm X in *Tree of Life*. I believe we have to get used to sharing our heroes, our creators, our important men and women, so as to have something with which to respond to the White world, which constantly hammers us with its values.

FP At that important Washington DC bookstore last night, you were saying that African-American heroes were also your heroes.

MC It was also my way of saying to people that I am tired of seeing them consider Francophone West Indians to be extraterrestrial beings. We must realize that we often share the same history.

FP In *Les derniers rois mages*, African-Americans are seeking a mythical Africa to which they try to reconnect by any means. You laugh at them, of course, but weren't you engaged in an identical quest in *Heremakhonon*? Even as you mock them, are you also laughing at yourself?

MC Yes, I laugh at myself. My quest is over. It ended with *Segu*. I ended it a long time ago, whereas they are still engaged in it. People have to understand one day that the quest must end and that they should live in the present.

FP In that same book you write the following about Debbie, when she returns to the United States after her liberating trip to the West Indies:

"She reencountered the prison of her race. She became George Middleton's daughter again, George Middleton, supposed martyr" [105]. Is race more of a prison for African-Americans than for West Indians or Africans?

MC I think so. In the final analysis I believe that, through no fault of their own, African-Americans live in a society that locks them inside their race. Everything is based on race, even the promotion of a book. You can't get away from it. When I promote a book in Paris, I go to all the radio stations – Europe 1, Luxembourg, France-Culture – and I also go, of course, to local Black stations. However, I don't go solely to Black radio stations, as is the case here.

FP While Spéro ponders the similarities between African-Americans and West Indians, the narrator humorously states, "The racist who said that all Blacks look alike was not that wrong after all" [185]. Can you elaborate on the similarities among Blacks in spite of their cultural differences? Is there a Black persona to be found among Blacks in Africa and in the diaspora?

MC When I first came to the United States and would go, for instance, to churches or supermarkets, I would see lots of faces that looked West Indian. People's clothes and hairdos were different but, physically, members of the Black Diaspora all look a little bit alike. What changes is people's relationship to themselves and their bodies, their behavior, their walk, how they come and go, but their physical traits are not unfamiliar to you. Since I haven't investigated further, I will limit myself here to visual observations. I don't know enough about the daily life of African-Americans to be able to explain these resemblances in more depth.

FP On October 24, 1992, while you were participating in a writers roundtable at the French Embassy in Washington DC, you said that people always put Black writers in an exotic ghetto, and that French literary critics often describe them as storytellers. You rebel against critics calling Black writers storytellers, yet you include the [African] oral tradition in your 1992 novel.

MC It's done intentionally. It was done as a search for a new narrative technique. It was done with a particular narrative style. I know that I belong to a civilization in which "oraliture" has held great importance over a long period of time. I want to rediscover this "oraliture," but I am not doing it in an instinctive fashion, by ear. I work on the language. I may integrate the tale into my narrative, but I am not writing tales. This search for technique and narrativity is never taken into account. People think Césaire used the spontaneous rhythm of Negro music to write *Return to My Native Land*. Césaire himself says that he spent years polishing his book. Some Black writers work hard on language and structure, a fact which is rarely acknowledged.

FP *Les derniers rois mages* has also been termed a "philosophical tale." What do you think of this definition?

MC I did not conceive it as such but as a rather structured narrative in which I placed different types of writing side-by-side and end-to-end, broke the narrativity and brought in the past. I didn't at all devise the work as a philosophical tale.

FP In a French regional newspaper, *Le Provençal*, dated April 12, 1992, the reviewer Jean-Rémi Barland wrote, "At once a historical, psychological, sociological, and mythological novel, as well as a private diary, this story of the new Magi reconciles the Black and the White peoples. More peaceful than the author's previous novels, *Les derniers rois mages* inscribes the history of the West Indies within a frantic search for brotherhood." What do you think about this comment?

MC The beginning about the different components is true, but to speak of "a frantic search for brotherhood" is perhaps a bit too much.

FP Has the reaction of French and Francophone critics to the book been generally favorable?

MC Quite favorable, on the whole.

FP Did they like the transposition of a period in the life of King Béhanzin, who was exiled by the French colonial power?

MC Yes, but sometimes they didn't really understand the novel. They would always use words like "exotic," "savory," and "humorous."

FP Last year you said that your favorite books were *Heremakhonon*, because it had been so heavily criticized, and *Crossing the Mangrove* because people always prefer their last-born. Should we assume that you currently [1992] prefer *Les derniers rois mages* over *Crossing the Mangrove*?

MC Yes. You can see that I follow a certain logic!

FP I recently came across your short story "Three Women in Manhattan" ("Trois femmes à Manhattan"), written ten years ago. I find it rather engaging, with its descriptions of New York City neighborhoods and portrayals of three Black women. One, the oldest, tried to become a writer but was never published, another succeeded in her literary career, and the third would like to write, but doesn't really dare to.

MC This short story is dedicated to Véra. She was an old Haitian woman who dreamed of becoming a writer. When I went to New York I used to spend the night at her place, and as happens in the story, she would read me all her unpublished manuscripts. There were plays and novels. One of the novels was titled "Les nuages en pyjama" (Clouds in pajamas).

FP What a surrealistic title!

MC There was something pathetic and ridiculous in the titles. These memories came back to me. At the time, I was just starting to write, so we were obviously at different points. Then I devised a third woman, Elinor, an established writer. In fact, the story took shape by itself in my head.

FP The story also includes another character, a young Guadeloupean woman, a recent immigrant, who does housecleaning for both the old lady and the successful author. . . .

MC And who wants to write. She thinks that one day she will write. This story is, in fact, about writing.

FP Is the title of one of Elinor's novels, "The Mouth That Eats Salt," a parody of Toni Cade Bambara's book *The Salteaters*?

MC No. I was thinking more about Ama Ata Aidoo and her play *The Dilemma of a Ghost*, in which there is a character named the Mouth That Eats Salt. I found the expression rather beautiful.

FP In your story Elinor exclaims, "They want me to speak once more about slavery and the slave trade and racism, for me to adorn us with the virtues of victims, and to inspire hope . . ." [Spear translation, 64]. She complains that readers and critics confine her to a particular genre and limit her freedom of expression. Does Elinor reflect your own feelings on that topic?

MC It's a trap that writers of the Black Diaspora often fall into because we have the misfortune of being published by the Other. The Other confines us to an image, perceives us in a particular way, and we don't always have the possibility of saying no and presenting ourselves differently. We need a lot of willpower and talent to arrive at this, so we very frequently endure pressures. However, it sometimes happens that these pressures lead to the type of commercial success we all dream of, and in the end you accept and give in. In the sentence you quoted, Elinor complains primarily about people in her own community who likewise demand that Black writers conform to certain canons. Black writers find themselves in a very difficult situation: on the one hand, they have their own people, those who read them locally and ask for and expect certain things; and on the other hand, there is the press, which creates literary success, objectifies, stresses exoticism, and asks for something else. In between these two types of demands, writers have to find themselves.

FP In addition, the narrator of the story compares writing to a "secret and remarkable alchemy" and to the delivery of a child: "To write! To put her hips, her sex, her heart into motion in order to give birth to a world inscribed in her obscurity" [59]. This is a very beautiful and essentially feminine image.

MC Yes, it is.

FP The narrator goes on to say about the old lady whose manuscripts were rejected, "Writing is but a trap, the cruelest of all, a snare, a sham of communication" [63]. Can you clarify this quote?

MC People never understand what you wanted to write. First, there is a misunderstanding: they expect one thing and are unhappy if you don't give it to them. You mean something and it's always distorted. People don't understand what you have meant and find multiple interpretations. Authors believe they give of themselves totally through writing, yet this dream of communication is never fulfilled.

FP This same story says about the young Guadeloupean, "She knew, however, that the audacity would come back to her . . . and that she would give birth to her world" [66]. Must one be daring in order to write?

MC It applies mainly to this young woman, who is a cleaning woman and is not well prepared for writing. She will have to overcome the fear of being intellectually incapable. Her job does not necessarily reflect her intellectual abilities. In short, people may clean houses because of difficult material circumstances, but they can have talent, even genius. She is an immigrant, she doesn't speak English very well, and it is therefore not her fault if she works at such a job.

FP "The Breadnut and the Breadfruit" ("La châtaigne et le fruit à pain"), published in 1988, is another short story that I have just been reading. The title comes from a West Indian proverb: "A woman is a breadnut, a man is a breadfruit." What does this proverb mean?

MC It means that a woman is tough and resilient, while a man is soft, spattering on the ground like a breadfruit. It's a West Indian proverb saying this, not I. "The Breadnut and the Breadfruit" is a short story about one of Etiennise's childhood memories. She remembers how her father charmed and pleased her as a girl, though he was actually a person without character. Her mother, on the contrary, was tough and strong, and she is the one who formed and influenced Etiennise. It has rather obvious symbolism based on a well-known popular saying.

FP Here, once again, the West Indian man is criticized?

MC I don't believe this is the case. Etiennise likes her father. She finds him charming and handsome; she is attracted to him and prefers him over her mother. It's only after her mother's death that she realizes how unfair she had been. Her father possesses a sort of charm, the art of attracting and pleasing. All the men I have described in my writings, from Spéro to John Indian and including Etiennise's father, are attractive. They know how to stimulate imagination, feelings, and senses! These are indeed positive qualities!

FP Etiennise is an ambiguous character. She has contempt for her mother, who raised her, and is fascinated by her father, whom she even serves as a go-between.

MC She does it without really knowing. She acts with innocence. She wants so much to please him that she'll do anything for him. In contrast, her mother is ugly, graceless, unloved, and in the end Etiennise rejects her. It is later, as we mentioned before, that she realizes that her mother had perhaps more positive qualities than her father.

FP Although I have not read it, I know you wrote "Victor et les barricades" (Victor and the barricades), which was published in 1989 in the children's magazine *Je bouquine*. What is it about?

MC It's the story of a boy who gets involved in riots. He is unsure of himself, rather attached to his mother, and weakhearted. In the midst of the riots he crosses the threshold of adolescence and asserts himself.

FP You have also written another children's story, *Hugo le terrible* (Hugo the terrible), in which you depict the aftermath of the hurricane that hit Guadeloupe several years ago. Has it been published? What is it about?

MC *Hugo le terrible* was published in 1990 by *Sépia*. It's the story of a child who is caught in a hurricane, lives through it, and tells about it in a diary. When the hurricane is over, he realizes it had become a part of him. Consequently, he feels quite empty. He has changed and grown, like Zazie [Raymond Queneau's fictional character].

FP Although he is not riding on the subway.

MC No, he was riding out a storm!

FP Several months ago, when I asked you your reason for writing, you answered that you were essentially writing for yourself. Yet you stated at the French Embassy that, like other West Indian writers, you were also writing to correct the inaccuracies people hold about the Caribbean. Have you changed your mind?

MC Not me personally. I was saying that a lot of writers wrote to rectify errors. I quoted Chinua Achebe, who started writing because he was so exasperated by the erroneous comments made about the Ibo people. This is not my case, because I don't write exemplary books, and I don't include exemplary situations and perfect characters in my works. As you said, my characters are often antiheroes, people who are not very sure of themselves and are not very likable.

FP These characters allow you to express certain ideas.

MC I like them because they often correspond to human situations I've encountered. Regarding *Tree of Life*, for instance, people have said that the Louis family members are not likable. They may not be, but the people from my family who inspired these characters were not likable either, yet I like them. I don't believe people have to be perfect to be liked. They are as they are.

FP You write a lot, you teach, you attend and participate in colloquiums, and you are currently involved in promoting the English translations of your latest books. Isn't it too much for one woman?

MC Oh, yes! In fact, I am trying to get out of promoting books.

FP How have your books been received in English? Do you have reactions yet to *I, Tituba, Black Witch of Salem* and *Tree of Life*?

MC So far, they have been very well received.

FP Do you find a difference in the ways European and American critics deal with your works?

MC You could say that the place where I really have a very faithful readership that understands me well, and where I receive rather nuanced critiques, is as small a country as Holland. Every time I go there, discussions and debates are in-depth and animated. I really feel that readers understand what I mean. In France, I always feel perceived in a somewhat exotic fashion. You should read the reviews of my books in French papers. For instance, my novel *Les derniers rois mages*, which is a rather sad book, is often termed a "humorous" and "savory" tale. In *Le Monde* there was a review entitled "Le Tim Tim de Maryse Condé," which means that the book was immediately associated with a tale from the West Indian oral tradition. In France I have a rather hard time counteracting the exotic fashion in which West Indian literature as a whole is perceived. In the United States, my works are seen in a more nuanced manner, but here literary critics aren't really familiar with the society I depict, which causes distortions in their appreciation of the works. However, in general, the gaze of American critics is less exotic than that of their French counterparts. African-American writers have trained U.S. critics not to treat books written by Blacks as special items to be judged differently. Because of these writers' reactions, American critics have become accustomed to considering African-American literature as part of literature per se. I think this makes them more respectful of the work. They don't automatically see it as an object of exoticism or entertainment.

FP We said a while ago that your books were translated into English in the United States and that you participated in colloquiums here. I feel that in France most people think of you mainly as the author of *Segu*.

MC Essentially.

FP It seems that in the United States your other works are taken much more seriously.

MC Yes, I agree. In France, writing a best-seller causes somewhat of a misfortune for the author. You have a hard time disengaging yourself from the image of an easy book that appealed to a large readership but was perhaps not very good as a literary work. All this obscures your subsequent production and prevents you from asserting yourself as a literary writer whose texts are written with a great deal of care and who must be recognized as a true creator.

FP And Americans don't label you that way?

MC No, because they think a best-seller is a good thing. It only means that the book appealed to a lot of people, and there is nothing wrong with that. Here, I don't feel it is infamous to have written a best-seller like *Segu*. And besides I don't know whether *Segu* is a best-seller in the United States. It is simply a book considered to be very important among certain African-American sectors. *Segu* hasn't had the notoriety in the United States that it had in France.

FP How would you compare your American students with your French students in the Caribbean literature classes that you teach?

MC American students know nothing about the subject. They discover things and listen to everything you tell them. They follow you, whereas French students usually have spent a vacation in the French Overseas Departments or in Africa, so they think they know it all. It is very hard to teach French students, because they believe they are more knowledgeable than you regarding Guadeloupe and Martinique. Here in the United States, people listen to you more modestly and thus profit more from classes.

Views on the Black Diaspora

7

FP How do Anglophone and Francophone West Indian literatures compare?
MC I think this question would require a very long discussion. Let's simply say that Francophone and Anglophone literatures were born in different ways. West Indian Francophone literature emerged from protest engendered by the Négritude movement, while Anglophone literature was born out of an immediate awareness of Otherness. The first Anglophone writers speak about their world, describe their relationship to this world, and make no attempt to define themselves in terms of the White world, the Western world. Obviously the White world is always present, but it is in the background; it is not immediately viewed as the world to which you want to compare yourself or to oppose.

Furthermore, issues of language are different in West Indian Anglophone and Francophone literatures. Problems related to Creolité and to people's relation to Creole languages, which are so acute in the Francophone areas today, are not the same in the Anglophone regions. This is perhaps because the Anglophone West Indies have had more freedom in crafting a language that integrates vestiges of the islands' past linguistic phases and stages. They have never experienced the terribly French exclusion of languages judged to be nonstandard or nonclassic. As a whole, it could be said that there are differences in themes as well as in the linguistic material itself.

FP You are in the process of preparing an anthology of West Indian literature. Does the book include primarily Francophone and Anglophone literatures, or does it also cover the literatures of former Dutch and Spanish islands?

MC At first we wanted to write an anthology of all these literatures to show strongly the diversity of the islands as well as their common problems. Unfortunately, this would have been too costly a project, and the publisher limited us to texts in French and English. We saw the differences between the various linguistic zones we've mentioned. We reached the conclusion that within their diversity, unity existed among the Caribbean islands, the affirmation of a personality that was neither African, nor American, nor European, to use the terms of the manifesto *Eloge de la créolité*. This personality was based on a common history and rather similar social and political evolution, an evolution that was more social than political. This year [1992], Anglophone West Indian literature has been crowned in an exceptional way with the awarding of the Nobel Prize to Derek Walcott. But it should be said that Naipaul, who is generally spurned because his work is not a celebration of West Indian culture, is a great writer whose complex books are written in a quite remarkable way. Spanish- and Dutch-speaking West Indian literatures are perhaps less known.

FP In 1983 you wrote an article on the Trinidadian writer Naipaul for *La Quinzaine littéraire*, in which you describe this writer of East Indian origin as someone who likes to irritate people, a bit like yourself. You conclude the article by writing, "In the final analysis he has ascribed another function to the writer, that of triggering despair and irritation in people at any cost rather than comforting them. Why?" Can you answer this "why?"?

MC I believe we live in a world that has a victimization complex. People like to comfort one another. It's not their fault if they are what they are. Naipaul simply felt like making a big splash by saying that victims were also guilty. I like this boisterous side of him. Naipaul writes this way in order to disturb good consciences. I think it is necessary as far as the West Indies are concerned.

FP Let's come back to your book project. What was your intention in writing this anthology? Is it a way for you, as a West Indian writer, to make a statement about West Indian literature?

MC It's a book aimed at the general public, to show that West Indian literature is very dynamic and that in spite of popular beliefs to the contrary, there isn't a wall between America and the West Indies. Certain themes in African-American literature can also be found in the West Indies, similar situations can exist, and the writers' work on language is not drastically different in these literatures. This anthology is a way to link the Americas with the Caribbean, which is so often overlooked, hidden, and forgotten.

FP In your opinion, who are the most representative authors of Anglophone West Indian literature?

MC We mentioned Derek Walcott and Naipaul. In addition, I would cite Wilson Harris, Edward Brathwaite, George Lamming, and Earl Lovelace. This literature written in English is flourishing and quite dynamic.

FP African oral traditions can be found in Africa's written literatures. What is the influence of oral literature on West Indian literature? What relationship do you have with oral literature in your works?

MC I can only speak for myself. I don't know West Indian oral traditions very well because I left the Caribbean at a very early age. Besides, even when I lived there, I was not exposed to the oral tradition. As we've already discussed, my parents were petit-bourgeois city dwellers, so I don't have intimate knowledge of the oral tradition. Yet I have always been aware of its existence. In my work I am striving to revive this oral tradition out of my own interest, through my own questioning, raising of issues, and research. I don't know it very well and am trying to reinvent it. Moreover, the oral tradition is hard to use as a starting point because, as we all know, it is threatened by television, the movies, and a totally modern lifestyle. You hardly know where to find it anymore. Writers such as myself, who weren't familiar with it in their childhood, must reinvent the oral tradition based on what remains of it and what we imagine it was in the past. It is a work of both re-creation and invention.

FP You were quoted in an interview conducted in the Netherlands as saying that your works reflected "the memory of things which never existed." Could you clarify this statement?

MC I would perhaps modify it and say "the memory of things which, to my knowledge, never existed." Not having intuitive consciousness or daily contact with West Indian oral literature, not having been raised in the warmth of orality, I can only imagine what it was and regret not knowing it better. I am making an effort to reconstitute it, based on my imagination and creativity.

FP Why aren't there more French-speaking West Indian poets? Is poetry a lesser genre as far as Francophone West Indian authors are concerned?

MC It's not a lesser genre. Quite the contrary, I think that poetry was raised to such a high level by Césaire and Saint-John Perse that people are a little afraid to enter the field and compete with these masters. However, in Guadeloupe there are quite a number of poets in French and Creole who try to publish their collections of poems. Poetry is not forgotten, although our era favors the novel because it corresponds to a period of reflection on the development of bourgeois and petit-bourgeois society.

FP How do you explain the small number of Francophone West Indian theatrical works?

MC The West Indies have not generated many plays, and I don't exactly know why. I can see that in Guadeloupe, for instance, there are some attempts being made in terms of theater with the Soubarou and Bakanal troupes. In order to write plays you have to see other plays, the same way you have to have read a lot in order to write a novel. While you can buy a book in the West Indies, plays are rarely performed there. So I believe that West Indian playwrights, confined to their islands, don't really have opportunities to see plays or compare their experiences with others. Their endeavors always remain somewhat limited in means and scope. They manage to obtain government subsidies and to stage plays. But theater needs to be strengthened through comparisons, and our playwrights don't go to the Avignon Theater Festival or see what the Comédie Française is all about. Such exposure is perhaps what West Indian playwrights lack. Insularity can be limiting.

FP In 1978 you ended your book on Césaire with the following words: "He is unquestionably the foundation of authentic West Indian literature" [71]. What do you think of this sentence in 1992?

MC I don't know whether I would say that now because I believe that there is no "authentic West Indian literature." I wrote these words fifteen years ago, and I have changed a great deal since. I now think that there is no such thing as "authentic" literature, that all literatures are valid, that everyone can express ideas, and that anyone has a right to express them, even though they may cause shock or displeasure. People who don't want to hear these things can always close the book they are reading. This being said, I would perhaps remove the word "authentic" from the sentence you quoted and would say that Césaire is the foundation of militant and committed literature, the kind of literature that speaks about the masses. It is in this sense that Césaire is the founder of literature in the French West Indies. His oeuvre is beautiful and eternal. Whatever people may think, no one has yet surpassed him in the West Indies.

FP But wasn't Césaire inspired by French surrealism?

MC Yes, but in the journal *Tropiques* he says that he used surrealism as a means rather than an end. He wanted to make use of surrealism to search for his own self and to recover his African essence hidden under the cloak of Western education, the same way the surrealists were looking for the primitive man, the child, hidden by education. He has thoroughly explained his relationship with surrealism, which involved a stylistic as well as a political rebellion.

FP In your book on Césaire, you established a difference between Cesairian and Senghorian Négritudes. Can you briefly speak about this?

MC These things are also quite dated. Négritude as a movement is no longer relevant. What is interesting now are other forces such as Antillanité and Créolité, which are currently at play in the French West Indies. The Négritude movement must be considered primarily from a historical viewpoint. It allowed Black people to assert themselves culturally, and we can indeed observe that Césaire and Senghor have not followed the same path. On the one hand, Senghor went back to Senegal and became president. His approach to Négritude boiled down to dividing the world between French and African people. On the other hand, Césaire has never considered Négritude from an ideological standpoint. For him Négritude is a literary and poetic movement.

FP In an article published in 1986, when Wole Soyinka was awarded the Nobel Prize for literature, you stated that Césaire deserved the award. Is this still your belief, now that Derek Walcott has just been awarded the Nobel?

MC I simply believe that at a time when the involvement of Blacks in literature is being recognized, Césaire should have been the first crowned. Given the beauty of Césaire's work and its importance in the world, it seems a bit unfair that Césaire has not received any international award consecrating his work.

FP Why was Derek Walcott awarded the Nobel Prize for literature? Does his work have more international impact than that of Césaire?

MC I don't have the slightest idea. I can't compare them.

FP Is Césaire's work as well known by non-Francophone people?

MC His work has been translated.

FP What do you think of Derek Walcott's work?

MC I only know his poem *Omeros*, which I find magnificent.

FP What will be the impact of Walcott's recognition in terms of the West Indies, West Indian literature, and the Black world?

MC I am told Walcott will go to Trinidad and Guadeloupe to celebrate his Nobel Prize, which means that West Indian people will perhaps be led to have greater confidence in their writers.

FP Patrick Chamoiseau, the Martinican writer, has just been awarded the Goncourt Prize for his novel *Texaco*. What do you think about his being selected? What are the characteristics of his work that may have led to the awarding of this highly coveted prize? Will this award result in making Patrick Chamoiseau a full-fledged French writer beyond the frontiers of Créolité?

MC I don't believe the Goncourt Prize will make a French writer out of Patrick. This award, which was given to him by the French literary world, will modify neither his writing nor his way of life as a Créolité writer. It's an award from the outside over which he has no control and which will not, in my opinion, influence him. His work contains an element that can be seen as "attractive" by French people: it involves a deconstruction of the French language that may appeal to them and that brings, as they say, spice and a certain zest to French as spoken in France. But I don't believe this is Patrick Chamoiseau's goal. I am convinced that his use of Creole, which is his mother tongue, responds to an inner need.

FP I found it paradoxical that the Goncourt Prize, which is a French award, was given to a work that tends to move away from standard French in its style.

MC It's because the French saw a renewal rather than a rejection of the French language in his work.

FP What will be the impact of the prize? Will French West Indian literature be taken more seriously? Will it be read more?

MC I think that it has already been taken seriously with such writers as Césaire and Glissant. However, I do believe it will be read more by the general public.

FP Chamoiseau is one of the bards of Créolité, a new literary movement extolled by writers from the French West Indies. What importance do you give to such a movement?

MC Créolité, which is the daughter of Antillanité, has many good points. It has allowed all West Indian writers to reevaluate their relationship to the French language. French is not the only language available to us; we also have Creole. However, Créolité should not be transformed into a cultural terrorism within which writers are confined. Créolité should not prevent individuals from having the relationship they wish to have with West Indian reality. To each his or her own Créolité, that is to say, to each his or her own relationship with oral materials and the oral tradition, and to each his or her own way of expressing it in written literature.

FP Don't you think Créolité may lead to exoticism?

MC It's a danger. You risk falling into the trap of appealing to the Other. Considering the fuss the French press is currently making about Francophone West Indian literature, one could indeed assume that this literature has exotic appeal. This may be dangerous, but if writers manage to keep their integrity in the midst of such a fashionable rage, they cannot be faulted.

FP Créolité is in the headlines, but Négritude is still appreciated and praised in many colloquiums, such as the one in Florida in 1987.

MC Césaire said that as long as there are Negroes there will be Négritude.

FP In your short story "Pays mêlé," we read that Georges, a bourgeois, despises reggae music, "a cacophony invented by the most dangerous of sects" [108]. Are popular musical forms such as zouk appreciated by all social classes in Guadeloupe and Martinique?

MC I believe zouk is appreciated by everybody. Musicians like Kassav are very popular.

FP Is there a political intention to promote West Indian music?

MC I don't see why politics should get involved in musical activities. Music is a cultural phenomenon that doesn't require efforts by Regional or General Council presidents. Private promoters set up concerts, organize tours, and send musicians and singers throughout the world. Politics has nothing to do with it. Could you imagine François Mitterrand sponsoring a tour by [the singer] Renaut? Music belongs to the creative realm. Where would we end up if politics got involved in it? Culture and politics should be independent. Let's let politicians do what they do, and do very poorly, and leave culture where it is!

FP Unlike Haiti, the French West Indies have no major artistic trend in painting and sculpture. Why not?

MC I am not very familiar with the issue of painting in the French West Indies as a whole, but I know that we have interesting painters in Guadeloupe, among them Michel Rovelas. He recently had an exhibition at the Pointe-à-Pitre Art Center, and we were impressed to see the level of maturity reached in paintings illustrating the "Discovery of the New World" theme. His work was very unusual from the point of view of colors and shapes. His painting style is not merely abstract and cannot be termed symbolic; it could be described as a bit of both: images that strike you very deeply without your really knowing why. You cannot immediately perceive the meaning of his paintings. You simply experience, as I mentioned before, a rather unusual feeling of both otherness and familiarity.

FP So in Guadeloupe there has actually been a shift away from the naive sort of painting that represented the heyday of Haitian art?

MC Absolutely. It's not at all the same style.

FP Let's move now from the West Indies to the United States. Which African-American authors interest you, as an author of the Black Diaspora?

MC I loved James Baldwin when I was young. *Go Tell It on the Mountain* is a book I've read several times, with passion. Above all, for me as a West Indian woman, the book had a novel theme in its relationship with God, its reinterpretation of God, and its way of addressing him in a very different language. The book also had something quite universal: a child who was ill-loved and unappreciated by his stepfather. These issues were also present in my consciousness, so I adored Baldwin. Later, I came to know the women writers whom everyone knows: Paule Marshall, Toni Morrison, Alice Walker. I loved them, yet I cannot say that I always identified with their writings. I always had the feeling that they wrote for a specifically African-American public of which I was not a part. Although it may sound a little pejorative, I must say that I didn't find in their works the same universality as in Baldwin.

FP What do you specifically like in Toni Morrison's works?

MC I particularly liked her first books, *The Bluest Eye* and *Sula*. I found her most recent works, *Beloved* and *Jazz*, somewhat hermetic in the way they were written. I think she went so far in her search for a specific writing style that these works are not easily accessible to a foreigner such as I. So I prefer the way Toni Morrison wrote at the beginning of her career.

FP What about writers like Richard Wright and Ralph Ellison?

MC I didn't like Richard Wright at all because of his didactic side, and I don't know whether Ralph Ellison moved me that much. I liked Ishmael Reed's *Mumbo Jumbo*. I didn't understand everything, but I could see that he tried to break the language apart and develop quite a different one. I was interested in all of his work on language and fictional style. "What is a novel?" he asks. Do we truly need models – Western or non-Western – or can we imagine the novel with a totally different form?

FP You have written several articles on African and West Indian cinema. Which African filmmaker do you prefer? In what direction does African cinema appear to be going?

MC My favorite African filmmaker is Ousmane Sembene, of course. I understand and approve of his ideological trajectory and his films. I share his thoughts concerning Africa, bourgeoisies, and the masses. I am also very interested in his relationship to language. I too wonder in what language we should address the common people in order to communicate with them. Can we speak to them? Can we bring them to listen to what we say? I also like Souleymane Cissé, although I haven't seen *Yeelen*. The Burkinabè school of cinema does not convince me. I have yet to see a film that would make me change my mind. I have the feeling that Burkina Faso's cinema is still very much yoked to a Western view of Africa. It has not yet found its autonomy and has not turned to its inner self in order to achieve authenticity.

FP What about cinema in the Ivory Coast?

MC I liked Henri Duparc's *Dancing in the Dust* (*Bal Poussière*) quite a bit. It really kept me in stitches, and I found it extremely amusing. I also enjoyed Désiré Ecaré's film *Faces of Women* (*Visages de Femmes*). Everybody was shocked by its erotic scene. I thought it was in fact the beginning of a freedom of tone and images that was quite unknown in African cinema, though it did stop with this film. I thought I was witnessing the end of militant African cinema and the birth of a personal, individual, and individualistic cinema.

FP Yet some people have said that Désiré Ecaré's cinema was not that personal and that his erotic scene catered to Western myths about African sexuality.

MC That's an easy and common criticism. I believe that human beings are human beings, and that they don't need to emulate the West in their lovemaking. People make love both in Africa and in Europe, and they take pleasure in bathing together in a river. I don't believe these traits are specifically Western. That line of thought reflects the facile criticism of false militancy.

FP Do you believe there is room for all sorts of African cinema?

MC I would perhaps like to see didactic, and entertaining, and thought provoking, and "author's" cinemas. I think it's a shame if cinema or literature isn't pluralistic.

FP In its thirty years of existence, have you noticed an evolution in Black Africa's cinema?

MC We spoke of Burkina Faso's cinema. I mentioned my slight regret that this much-celebrated school was, in effect, supervised by the French, both technically and financially, and perhaps also at the level of its portrayal of Africa.

FP What about West Indian cinema?

MC There is barely anything apart from the work of Euzhan Palcy.

FP What about Christian Lara?

MC I think he has not been producing anything for a long time. He generated a fair amount of hope with *Coco la Fleur Candidat* (Candidate Coco la Fleur), but he hasn't really kept his promise. There is Euzhan Palcy. I was rather fond of her first film, *Sugar Cane Alley* (*Rue Cases-Nègres*), because it was a story I knew by heart. Like all French West Indians, I had read the book on which it is based, *Black Shack Alley*. From characters to landscapes, you have the feeling that the film portrays the society to which you belong. Its chronicling of the past was very appealing.

FP What do you think about François Migeat's *Le sang du flamboyant* (Blood of the flamboyant tree), another French West Indian film?

MC I saw this film quite a while ago. It was one of the first West Indian films I saw. It obviously generated an impression of discovery. All of a sudden I saw West Indian characters and scenes brought to life, not in a folkloric way, as I had seen in documentaries by French directors. I remember most of all that a very beautiful scene showed the illumination of a cemetery. But I think that *Le sang du flamboyant* is an isolated case, and to my knowledge François Migeat has not shot another film.

FP You recently mentioned to me a new West Indian film made by a woman, Christiane Goldman-Succab.

MC Yes, people often ask my opinion of West Indian cinema. I would say that it is still in the process of being born. You cannot say it has truly emerged yet. Christiane's movie, a reflection on hurricane Hugo, is a film with depth. It is a documentary that is also fiction. It offers West Indians a way to rediscover themselves, speak about themselves and their reality in the wake of the huge destruction wreaked by the hurricane. The film is poetic but also shows social reality. It's a very interesting work, but as we say, "One robin does not the spring make," and I don't believe we can validly talk yet about a Francophone West Indian cinema.

FP What do you think of Anglophone West Indian films, such as *The Harder They Come*?

MC It wasn't bad, especially since it had a beautiful musical score. And the plot was quite charming: a young man has his musical compositions stolen from him, so he becomes an outlaw. It was quite beautiful, but "one film does not a cinema make."

FP What do you think of African-American films?

MC I am most familiar with Spike Lee's movies, which I have never cared for very much. I've always been shocked by his depiction of women, racially mixed couples, music, and the world of musicians. I don't think there is a single Spike Lee film that didn't shock me in some way. I was probably most disappointed with his last film, *Malcolm X*, because I greatly admire Malcolm X, whom I saw in Ghana. I expected, perhaps naively, the creation of a Malcolm X myth, but I found the film quite confusing in its presentation of the hero. The different parts of his life were treated so unevenly that the image of Malcolm doesn't give people a clear idea about him. For instance, the first part, when Malcolm was a drug dealer and pimp, is very long. It seems like Spike Lee enjoyed shooting the dancing and musical part, which is also very caricatured and lengthy. Then the last part, when Malcolm X changed and began to seriously think about the problems of Blacks and Whites, is, of course, passed over. And in typical Hollywood fashion, the middle sections are very superficial and don't really deal with the problems of his relationship to Black Muslims and revolution in America.

FP So you believe it is not a film that will enlighten people who don't know Malcolm X or don't know him well?

MC I don't know, but as far as I am concerned, I had an image of Malcolm X derived from Alex Haley's book about him, and I didn't find the character I loved in the film.

FP Isn't there a Spike Lee movie you prefer over the rest?

MC Maybe *Do the Right Thing* appealed to me more than the others because it is less didactic, more nuanced. It introduces viewers to several different ways of living and being in the United States. There are no merely good or merely bad characters in the film. Even the Italian pizzeria owner, who eventually provokes the riot, is first presented as a rather congenial character who believes he knows the people living around him. I think I preferred this film because of its nuances.

FP Has anyone asked about adapting your novels for the screen?

MC Yes, people ask all the time. The Algerian filmmaker Rachid Bouchareb has made a serious offer to adapt *Segu*.

FP Are you working with him on this project?

MC I am working with him on the film script. I mainly deal with the dialogue. I make the characters speak, trying to translate the whole book into dialogue. It is long and arduous because you have to draw out dialogue from the narrative and the characters' thoughts. And film dialogue is different from a book: words have to lend themselves to being spoken without being too colloquial. You have to find a certain tone. How do you have El Hadj Omar speak? In the book, he speaks in a very solemn way that would be unsuitable for the screen. He cannot talk like you and I do either, so you have to find a middle ground between commonplace and pompous words.

FP Is your collaboration fruitful in spite of differences in generation and culture?

MC We have met several times and have cooperated in a collective fashion. I am sure we will achieve very satisfying results.

FP Are you also in the process of writing a new novel?

MC Yes, it is practically finished, and I am going to send it to the publisher soon.

FP What is it about?

MC As a rule, I don't like to speak about my novels before they are published.

FP When will it be published?

MC Robert Laffont will bring it out in the summer of 1993.

FP Can we at least have the title?

MC *La colonie du nouveau monde* (The colony of the New World).

From "Comédie d'amour" to
La colonie du nouveau monde

WASHINGTON DC, FEBRUARY 9, 1994

8

FP Since our last meeting in 1992, your play "Comédie d'amour" has been staged in France and the United States, and your novel *La colonie du nouveau monde* has been published. The Guadeloupean troupe Plus Bakanal presented the play in Washington DC on October 9–10, 1993. Who sponsored the actors' visit?

MC No one person or organization sponsored it. A number of people showed interest in the play: ACRA [a local association of French West Indians], the French Embassy, and the University of Maryland, which offered support for publicity. These three entities contributed to bringing the play here.

FP How was the play received?

MC I think there was a sense . . . I wouldn't want to say of *exoticism*, which is negative, but rather of surprise. This was apparently the first time people here had seen a theater troupe direct from Guadeloupe, with Guadeloupeans who spoke in a certain way and used certain body language. And they didn't present broad issues such as racial problems and the exploitation of man by man. They showed the problems in their society: the relationship between men and women, and the difficulty in making a relationship work. I think people were captivated by these aspects of the play and reacted favorably, especially students and young people. So, generally speaking, "Comédie d'amour" was well received.

FP I spoke to people who found your play surprising when compared with your published works of fiction. As a play, "Comédie d'amour" seemed rather light to them.

MC I wrote the play for Plus Bakanal, which is a comedy troupe; in fact it is Guadeloupe's best-known comedy troupe. José Jernidier, a longtime friend with whom I have worked on a number of projects, asked me to write a text for his company. I couldn't give him something tragic or hopeless. So, I had to adapt, and obviously the tone of this play is very different from what I usually write.

FP Do we have here the formula for West Indian popular theater, a theater for the people?

MC I don't wish to propose a formula at all. It was a one-time experiment that interested me and was a bit of a challenge. But if this were to become customary, I would no longer be interested. If I ever work with Plus Bakanal again, it will be on something quite different. But we have no plans at the moment.

FP The play appears to be humorous, but it deals with very serious themes, such as the alienation of West Indian women and problems arising from the generation gap.

MC People who saw the play here said that it didn't necessarily have to be performed as a farce. "Comédie d'amour" can be performed in a serious mode, a solemn mode. Plus Bakanal is used to performing heavy comedy for West Indian audiences, so they played it that way.

FP In Washington, people seemed to view the play as more serious than in Paris, where there was a lot of interaction between the actors on stage and the audience. Everyone was laughing.

MC That's because in Paris, as in Guadeloupe and Martinique, only West Indians saw it. In Paris there is a sort of . . . I wouldn't say racism, but snobbishness, which makes people not go to see a Guadeloupean popular play. There was practically no press coverage, except for one article in *Le Parisien* that was rather paternalistic and said, "West Indians act at the theater like they would at a puppet show" and such. Parisian snobbishness is such that a play like "Comédie d'amour" cannot draw serious attention from the critics. The audience was made up of West Indian expatriates, and they had the same reactions as Guadeloupeans and Martinicans living in the West Indies.

FP They were back in their own environment again. . . .

MC Exactly. They already knew the troupe because it had performed its collectively written play *Moun Koubari* (People of Koubari) the year before. They were used to the actors; they laughed; in a sense they were at home.

FP "Comédie d'amour" was also presented last fall in New York. How was it received there?

MC There were mainly Haitians in attendance at the Alliance Française since, as we all know, the Haitian community in New York is quite large. A few French and American people went, but the majority of the audience was Haitian. They reacted just like other West Indians, Guadeloupeans, or Martinicans. The play was well received there.

FP Joyfully?

MC Joyfully. The French people in the audience were a bit surprised by this sort of West Indian spectacle, which they are not accustomed to seeing.

FP You told me once that your plays addressed both French and West Indian audiences. But in Paris, people who did not know Creole found it a little frustrating not to understand some of the dialogue. What could an author do to make a play completely accessible to both?

MC I believe that the French who said they didn't understand the play's Creole didn't really make an attempt. Creole is not that hermetic for a French person, who can at least guess at what is being said. If you link it to the dialogue in French and follow the situations and gestures, you can easily understand. "Comédie d'amour" has perhaps a lot of Creole, "grassroots" Creole, we might say, but I believe that if French people had made an effort, they would have been able to follow a play written in both French and Creole.

FP I must say that I myself was lost at times when people spoke Creole in the play, particularly when the two male actors engaged in an extended dialogue. Everybody was laughing, and it was frustrating for me not to understand.

MC Maybe that part was slightly too long. An author should see to it that small bridges in French appear in the dialogue from time to time.

FP Don't you think that, in this context, Creole somewhat limits the universal appeal of a play?

MC If people see a play performed in English, in Spanish, or in German, they don't ask that question. So why would Creole limit the universalism of a play? Creole is like any other language. You have to make an effort to understand it, cock your ear and try to get it. I wonder if this is once again some sort of prejudice against Creole.

FP And against the West Indies?

MC Well, let's say against Creole.

FP I understand that you don't necessarily wish to continue with this type of popular West Indian theater, but do you plan to write other theater pieces?

MC I've never planned to write a play. Each time it has been for a particular purpose, either for Sonia Emmanuel, for whom I wrote a play, or because the Regional Council or Plus Bakanal asked me to. There may be other occasions like these in the future, but right now I am not planning to do other plays.

FP Has the experience of working with Plus Bakanal brought you something in terms of your general approach to theater? Has working with a troupe modified your approach to drama?

MC I didn't work with them that much. We read through "Comédie d'amour" several times before I left Guadeloupe. I made a few suggestions concerning casting. José had selected actors whom I didn't really like, so I expressed some reservations about them. During the readings I changed the dialogue whenever words didn't roll off the actors' tongues. But after I left for the States, the actors worked alone. I saw them only after the product was finished.

FP They are not professional actors?

MC No, they are not.

FP What do they do?

MC José, the director, teaches computer science. One of the young women is an optician. I believe another one is a housewife. One of the men is a night watchman and another is unemployed. It was really the common people of Guadeloupe on stage.

FP Your most recent novel, *La colonie du nouveau monde*, carries two epigraphs. One is taken from the "Great Hymn to Aton," which is engraved on the walls of a tomb in Egypt. Aton is the name of your protagonist, the sun worshipper. Who was the real Aton of Ancient Egypt?

MC I wasn't really interested in the history of Egyptian religion. I leafed through a few books and noticed that a solar revolution had been carried out by one of the Egyptian pharaohs named Aton. He took the place of the sun, he became the Sun God, and put himself in the pantheon of the gods. That's all I was interested in. It's not a book on Egyptian religion, and I would not be able to give details on Aton's revolution. I simply know that he forced the clergy to consider him not merely the representation of a god, but the very Sun God, an avatar of the Sun God.

FP In your novel, Aton is a wanderer who searches for himself in an endless quest, whereas in Ancient Egypt Aton was a glorious pharaoh. Is this an ironic view of your character?

MC No, I was fascinated by the literature surrounding Aton, all the hymns and prayers, which were truly beautiful. They were compiled in a book on Egyptian religions by the African historian Theophile Obenga. I plunged into Obenga's book and all this inspired me, giving me the idea to rediscover this religious literature and reacquaint people with it. In *La colonie du nouveau monde*, all of Aton's incantatory words are authentic. I excerpted them from Obenga's work.

FP The second epigraph in your novel is a quote from the Guyanese writer Wilson Harris: "When one dreams, one dreams alone. When one writes a book, one is alone." With this epigraph, are you establishing a link between Wilson Harris's work and your own?

MC What I like primarily in Wilson Harris's work is his allusion to dreams. Let's say that a novel is a dream that you have. I wanted to react against the totalitarian and collective notion of the novel that people have in the West Indies. They imagine that the novel must obey certain rules. People cast the novel in a particular mold and constantly say, "The novelist should do this, the novelist shouldn't do that." In his own way, Wilson Harris demanded creative freedom. Novelists do what they want.

FP In the West Indies, people generally insist that novels be socially oriented.

MC Yes, with references to political and social problems. Novels must contain historical markers. Edouard Glissant has said that history must be rewritten; whoever doesn't rewrite history has failed in his mission. But all these dictates, all these commandments, limit the novelist's scope.

FP Does the novel, as dream, reflect the author's subconscious?

MC I believe that someone, whose name escapes me, said that "a novel is a subconscious made naked." You start with a particular idea, and you don't even know where it comes from. It imposes itself on you. I think that three-quarters of the writing of a novel, the organization of the narrative, and the sketching of characters come from our subconscious.

FP So, if people really analyzed a work, they would eventually penetrate the author's subconscious?

MC This is what most critics do, in fact.

FP Could you briefly summarize *La colonie du nouveau monde*, which, like some of your other works, deals with the experiences of wanderers?

MC This novel was inspired by a friend whose life destiny is not as tragic as that of my characters. She was an actress who never got to play roles in France that were up to her level. She subsequently quit acting and had a child. Building on these facts, I imagined that she was so disappointed that she not only lived with a guy, which is a happy situation, but also renounced the type of life she had led. Is this guy, named Aton, insane? Is he some sort of "enlightened one"? You don't really know; he is never clearly defined. With him, she takes refuge in the dream of recreating an Ancient Egyptian religion that would be much more tolerant and warmer than the ones we know.

First, they go to Guadeloupe to start a religious community, which lasts a few years. They have followers; they have children. The community flourishes, but then the "colonial power" butts in and forces them out. They seek shelter at the home of a *béké* and then – the book begins here – settle on the Caribbean coast of Colombia. I purposely selected this coastal region to show that it belongs to our universe and that we must not sever Guadeloupe from this culture, which extends throughout the Caribbean region and Latin America, the whole American continent, in fact. The characters are there, waiting for a boat that is expected, theoretically, to take them to Egypt. The boat doesn't come. Finally, the whole community disintegrates. Some die; others end up in jail. Everything turns out wrong except for a young girl who is sent back to Guadeloupe to join her mother's bourgeois family.

FP But does the novel really end the right way? With their new religion, the girl's parents tried to escape the conventional world, which they rejected. If their daughter returns to her mother's roots, to a totally bourgeois and conventional context, is this a good ending?

MC Therein lies the irony. Her parents sought an escape from the world. In the final analysis the world defeated them. Their child goes back. Questions can be raised. You can very well imagine that this child, arriving in Guadeloupe, might find herself reabsorbed into the system and structure that her mother had detested. Therein is the whole ambiguity. I think endings must be open so that everyone raises questions.

FP The way the novel ends suggests that the plane carrying the little girl back to Guadeloupe may crash.

MC The little girl, Meritaton, is frightened. It's her first trip on a plane, and in addition she is defying a prohibition by her father, who did not want his followers to travel by plane. So of course she is doubly frightened. Yet I was careful not to suggest a precise ending. Free rein should be given to the imagination. Readers are interested in what occurs after the book ends. When I go to speak in schools, children always ask me, "But what happens afterward?" I answer, "What comes afterward depends on you. You must invent what happens." I think the novelist's role is to open up possible alternatives so that readers use their imagination.

FP Meritaton's death would certainly stress the hopeless side of the novel. . . .

MC As far as I am concerned, she doesn't die. In my view she is scared, she is terrified: the plane, the clouds, the turbulence. I see her going back to Guadeloupe and beginning a new novel.

FP A new novel . . . the one you are currently writing?

MC No, it's a novel that has nothing to do with what I am now writing, but which I could write.

FP The title of your latest book refers to its geographic location, the New World, but also to the new world that Aton wants to build. Which one of these new worlds prevailed in your mind while you were writing *La colonie du nouveau monde*?

MC If I had worked a bit faster, *La colonie du nouveau monde* would have been published in 1992, the year of the quincentenary of Christopher Columbus's arrival in the Americas. For me it was a way to mock things by saying, "Well, here is a new world, the New World Columbus discovered with ecstasy and amazement because he thought these were marvelous islands where everything was beautiful and where the whole world could begin again. . . ." Everyone knows that our New World is rather sad and hopeless. There are problems in Central and South America, to say nothing of the United States and the Caribbean. So, it was a sort of parable on the state of our world, an ironic wink. But unfortunately I dragged it out too much and didn't finish on time, so *La colonie du nouveau monde* was published in 1993, at a time when people were no longer talking about Christopher Columbus.

FP Why did you decide to set most of your novel in Colombia?

MC I wanted to broaden the scope of the West Indian novel in any way possible. I believe I have already said that I find it boring for a Martinican to talk only about Martinique, for a Guadeloupean to talk only about Guadeloupe, and for a Guianese to talk only about French Guiana. I think we definitely have the right to speak of other lands. In addition, I think that Colombia, especially its Caribbean coast, experienced a history similar to ours: the arrival of African slaves, their settlement on plantations, slave rebellions, runaway slave communities, and the like. If you look at this culture, you notice that it is syncretic and pluriethnic like that in the West Indies. Moreover, Colombia is a magic land, it is García Márquez's land, and you have the feeling that by speaking about it, you get closer to him.

FP Colombia's landscapes and ambiences are extremely well described in *La colonie du nouveau monde*. Have you visited that country?

MC I haven't actually been to Colombia. I traveled in my imagination, and I do think that imagination is the best possible guide.

FP The concept of a curse or malediction appears in *Crossing the Mangrove* in the Francis Sancher character, whose ancestors committed the sin of slaveholding. A similar notion of malediction is found in works of the Mexican writer Octavio Paz. In his *Labyrinth of Solitude*, Mexicans are defined as the illegitimate offspring of the rape of Indian women by the conquistadors. Have you read this book?

MC Yes, I read it with great interest. I even use it in my classes, because, although Octavio Paz talks specifically about Mexicans, what he says is valid for all colonized people. It could be applied to West Indians or Africans. But I don't believe I actually thought about Octavio Paz while writing *La colonie du nouveau monde* or *Crossing the Mangrove*. Of course, it is difficult to say whom you thought about while writing a book. A lot of references surface unconsciously.

FP Several Latin American writers incorporate family sagas into their works, as do you. I am thinking in particular of *Tree of Life* and *Les derniers rois mages*. Your family sagas are somewhat reminiscent of *House of the Spirits* by Isabel Allende, of Chile. Do you enjoy her works?

MC I liked *House of the Spirits* a lot, but I wouldn't say it influenced me. A sort of brotherly – or should I say sisterly – relationship can certainly be found between *House of the Spirits* and *Tree of Life*. This year I experimented with a course entitled "Do women of the Americas have a common literature?" I selected Allende, Marita Golden . . . and of course *Tree of Life*. However, I cannot say that I consider Isabel Allende a major writer. It seems to me that as a writer, she is less comprehensive, less accomplished than García Márquez.

FP This interest that you and Latin Americans have shown in the theme of filiation: is it linked to the fact that you are all writers from former colonial societies, writers attempting to reconstruct your historical, social, and cultural heritage through fiction?

MC Perhaps. I also believe that the family remains the essential element in our societies and social fabric. Whatever you do, you are still someone's daughter; you are defined by a particular genealogy. People always feel the need either to distance themselves from the family or to become an integral part of it; there is no getting away from this. It's true that a number of writers in the Americas engage in a symbolic search for the reality that existed before the rape of slavery. But I believe that more important are the preeminence of the family nucleus and the constant need to define yourself in terms of that nucleus.

FP This identity-related search for a mythic past and a better world is found in *La colonie du nouveau monde*, *Heremakhonon*, and *Les derniers rois mages*. This approach seems different from that of Edouard Glissant, who recently stated on France-Inter radio that he refuses to engage in any inventory of origins.

MC Glissant seems to refuse such an inventory now. However, a few years back he was saying that you cannot exist if you don't know your past, that without knowledge of the past, you have no present. This contradiction doesn't shock me. It's part of the writer's thought processes.

FP At one point in the past, you spoke of the difference between Anglophone and Francophone West Indian literatures, but you didn't mention Hispanophone West Indian literature. What characterizes it?

MC I know very little about it. I am familiar with only two Puerto Rican women writers: Ana Lydia Vega and Rosario Ferré. Ana Lydia Vega writes short stories, and Ferré has written several novels. Such is the extent of my knowledge. I cannot draw conclusions based solely upon what they have written.

FP In his novel *The War of the End of the World*, the Peruvian author

Mario Vargas Llosa illustrates the tragic end of a religious community in Brazil, which the government decided to eliminate in 1897. As in *La colonie du nouveau monde*, the community is headed by a prophet whose values contrast sharply with those of the dominant society. Have you read *The War of the End of the World*?

MC No, I haven't read this book. What I like in Mario Vargas Llosa's work are the erotic novels. One must admit, however, that the story in *La colonie du nouveau monde* is commonplace and even banal. Sects proliferate in the world in which we live. These sects have prophets who think they can change everything. The result is usually violent – bloodshed and fire. These are themes, images, and stories that can easily haunt a writer's imagination.

FP You met Rastas during your trip to Jamaica in 1980, and there are Rasta communities in Guadeloupe. Did they inspire you at all in your latest novel?

MC Yes, I have always been quite interested in Rastas. If you look at what I have written since *Tree of Life*, you will notice that Rastas are always included.

FP Why?

MC Because I find it fascinating to see people who want to change life, who have an ideal and the desire to transform society, who are tired of the world we experience each day. I have already mentioned that I even spent three days in a Rasta community in Jamaica. In Guadeloupe there is also the Jah family, whom I went to visit in Capesterre.

FP Is the Jah family a Rasta community?

MC No, because most of the disciples have left. Only the father, Adam Jah, the mother, Eve Jah, and the children have remained. There are also two followers who help run errands and farm the land. The Jah family certainly impressed me. I learned that they had lived for a while on the land of a *béké*, who had such a guilt complex about slavery that he sheltered them for a while . . . before kicking them out. I thought about all this when I made Aton's family seek refuge at the white planter's.

FP Is the Caribbean region prone to religious sects, given its mix of religious faiths?

MC No, I don't believe so. I think Latin America and the United States are very propitious terrains for such sects. All you need are populations that experience acute political and social problems and are at the same time influenced by religion. If, in addition, the society has always extolled a religious discourse, in total contradiction to its social practice, this produces an explosive situation.

FP It's interesting to see that you wrote *La colonie du nouveau monde* between the tragic cult-related events that took place in Jamestown, Guyana, and more recently in Waco, Texas. Do writers have antennas? Do they sometimes foresee events? Isn't it a bit troubling to write a novel and then witness, for example, what happened in Waco?

MC I completed my novel at the beginning of February, and I believe Waco occurred at the end of March. I remember telling Richard, "Everybody is going to think I copied Waco." In fact, writers often have visions that foreshadow reality. Chinua Achebe said that he had written novels that anticipated coups d'état or wars that occurred later in Nigeria. I think that by constantly questioning what goes on around them, writers end up with the gift of foresight.

FP In *La colonie du nouveau monde*, Aton and his disciples are rejected by other people. How do you explain the rejection of nonconformists in contemporary industrial societies?

MC Nonconformists scare people. All these people who refuse technology, who refuse a certain form of consumer society, are considered dangerous. It is feared they may have the power to destroy the established order.

FP Aton spent some time in a psychiatric ward. Now he celebrates a religion acquired through self-instruction, hence certain dangers. James Jones and David Koresh were also accused of being megalomaniacal madmen who surrounded themselves with people lacking direction. Is Aton to be seen as the archetypal religious leader whose mysticism borders on insanity?

MC I had to leave readers in doubt concerning the character's true nature. Obviously, scientific views of such individuals are totally negative. But people who believe in them regard them as gods and divine reincarnations. These are people who cannot be judged objectively because they are perceived through different subjectivities. Aton's psychiatrist says that he is mentally ill. His disciples Mandjet and Mesketet say he is a god. His wife Tiyi doesn't voice any opinion as to what he is. All of this is done so that readers may reach their own conclusions.

FP Although he is introverted and lives on dreams and chimeras, Aton's sincerity is rather moving. He believes in the Sun God, but when he feels forsaken by this god, he decides to end his life. Aton is certainly a pathetic character, yet he is neither a profiteer nor a scoundrel. Moreover, you compare him to Christ, writing that he was "alone, desperately alone, like Christ on the Mount of Olives" [135]. Isn't there not only some insanity in him but also an undeniable purity?

MC I didn't really ask myself questions about Aton. I simply wanted to make a sort of avatar of Christ. He is forsaken by everyone. Still, it should be recognized that he is rather empty as a character. He pronounces only words set in prayers. All the gestures he makes are automatic. So, just who is he? I took great care not to say, leaving each reader free to fill him with insanity or mysticism. Actually he is somewhat of a mask.

FP In your novel, Aton and a number of other people tried to change the world and failed. Do you think that it is impossible to change the world at the present time?

MC It's difficult, though I won't say it is impossible. I think that in all the novels I have written there is always this sad observation: people who want to change the world fail. Is it an impossible task? Do people go about it in the wrong way? Will we succeed later in such endeavor? I don't know. I only notice that revolutions have never brought truly lasting and positive improvements in the condition of peoples.

FP If changing the world is impossible, should we escape from it?

MC Maybe, though it is difficult to escape. This is why, at the end of the novel, Meritaton, the little girl, goes back to her mother's family. This means that bourgeois society always has the last word. People want to escape from this society, but in the final analysis it always gets you back. People detest the capitalist regime of the United States, yet this country is now helping Russia and will perhaps send planes to Bosnia-Herzegovina and restore peace there. Like it or not, bourgeois and capitalist societies end up having the last word.

FP In *La colonie du nouveau monde*, as in your other works, many of your characters seem to be doomed to wandering and wishing to be where they are not. Is this constant search for a Promised Land the distinguishing feature of human beings? Since this Promised Land doesn't exist, should we see this search as life's ultimate chimera?

MC I think we should.

FP How did you get the idea of creating the character of Enrique, the communist Santa Marta councilman and Don Quixote of modern times?

MC I don't really know. Enrique seems to be a character you frequently encounter in our world. He believed in a Marxist ideology. It failed. He remains extremely good-hearted, yet he doesn't know very well what to do with this goodness. At the same time he is very weak. He lacks morals in his relationships with women. It seems that I am surrounded by dozens of people like him. I simply depicted a character I know.

FP Tiyi, the novel's central female character, reminds me of Veronica and Marie-Hélène in *Heremakhonon* and *A Season in Rihata*.

MC Someone blamed me for Tiyi's passivity. I don't agree with this perception. I wanted to depict a woman who has run out of steam, a woman who has tried everything, failed, and is simply waiting for the end to come. I think that when people reach a state of anguish or extreme despair, they don't have the courage to act. Readers always want fictional characters to be positive heroes. I don't think this is possible. Tiyi, Veronica, and Marie-Hélène may be the same kind of heroines. They can be called Condé's heroines.

FP Are you Tiyi?

MC Certainly not!

FP Unlike the Guadeloupean writer Myriam Warner-Vieyra, who includes the theme of insanity in several of her novels and short stories, you introduce it for the first time in *La colonie du nouveau monde* with Tiyi. Is the mental illness into which she descends the ultimate reflection of her psychological and spiritual drifting?

MC Tiyi goes insane when her child dies, when she is told about the drowning death of her daughter. Even before that, Tiyi was on her last breath. To use colloquial terms, her daughter's death is the drop of water that triggers her insanity. It is a refuge from extreme dissatisfaction and failure. Women taking refuge in insanity can be found, for instance, in Charlotte Brontë's *Jane Eyre* and in Jean Rhys's *Wide Sargasso Sea*, in the Antoinette Bertha Cosway character. It's a constant in women's literature. Unable to express herself as she wishes, the woman finds refuge in suicide, death, or insanity.

FP Does the woman find refuge in insanity, or is it that insanity seizes her mind? One cannot say that people choose insanity!

MC You do not choose insanity, but you may welcome it as a blessing. It is plausible that when these characters reach a state of insanity, they attain a form of liberation.

FP Most of the Black and White characters in *La colonie du nouveau monde* are the shipwrecked of life, who try to cling to a religious ideology. In fact this work is rather pessimistic, given its deaths, suicides, and insanity. Your book also expresses dreams, premonitions, and the force of destiny. Having all these elements, your novel sounds a bit like an Ancient Greek tragedy. *La colonie du nouveau monde* is one of the strongest but also one of the most pessimistic novels that you have written. Is this still linked to your disenchantment as a writer that you mentioned in 1991?

MC A book reflects a moment, a passing state of mind. It is possible that while writing this book in 1991–92, I was plunged into a desperate lucidity. A book is the photograph of a moment. Maybe at the time I didn't have much faith in the future of our societies, in the possibility of individuals surviving the total deterioration in relations between human beings and between societies.

FP Did you pattern the characters Ute and Rudolf after the hippies of the 1960s?

MC Not at all. When I went to see the Jah family in Capesterre, a young German couple was visiting them. The woman wore her hair braided with pearls, and the young man had blue eyes. They both impressed me and made me think, "This is rather incredible: two young Germans who leave Berlin to come and meet Jah and Eve, both of whom are terribly lost!"

FP One of your other characters, a Haitian by the name of Thoutmès, used to draw crowds of destitutes in his country because out of his mouth "rolled words that gave birth to the desire to act" [110]. Was he preaching a type of liberation theology? What do you think of this concept, which has appeared in parts of Latin America?

MC I have no opinion whatsoever because I know very little about it. I haven't truly given much thought to it. What appealed to me regarding Thoutmès, as well as Aristide, was his effort to challenge fate. People always thought that Haitian Blacks had no access to political power, that they could not voice their opinion in the government of their country. For once, a president, Aristide, came to power and said, "Fok sa changé!" – "This must change!" In *La colonie du nouveau monde*, Aristide is split in two. On the one hand, you have the president who is of course never seen. On the other, you have Thoutmès. This is my way of paying homage to Aristide's words.

FP Thoutmès seems to use rather negative terms when he talks about

Aristide. He thinks Aristide is a false prophet [144] and speaks of his "moustache and dying eyes" [160], which is not a very flattering description. . . .

MC To have "dying" eyes is a positive trait. It means having great big, slightly sad eyes, like a deer's. Thoutmès is quite attached to the president. Remember that he went to school with him. I think he likes him a lot.

FP Does Aristide interest you as a character?

MC Aristide does not interest me at all as an individual. But he also represents this: a fragile little man who comes with a revolutionary discourse. He loses and has to go into exile, but he doesn't acknowledge defeat. He tries in vain to come back. . . . This is a symbol that appeals to me in a literary sense.

FP In this and other novels you refer frequently to Haiti. Here, for instance, you describe Port-au-Prince as a "city of suffering, mourning and death" [146]. You also mention the communities of Haitians in U.S. and European cities, "all places where Haiti's poverty is spreading" [180]. Do you have a special feeling for Haiti?

MC I have always considered Haiti a country of great misfortune. I started making Haitian friends as early as 1957, when I was a student. I participated in the first anti-Duvalier demonstrations in Paris in 1958. My interest in Haiti goes back years.

FP Now, if you agree, let's talk about another aspect of *La colonie du nouveau monde*. It seems to me that sexual references and connotations are more numerous here than in your other novels.

MC I don't think this novel has more sexual connotations than *Heremakhonon*, *Crossing the Mangrove*, or *Les derniers rois mages*.

FP But the sex in *La colonie du nouveau monde* is rather sordid: adultery, prostitution, incest, sodomy, ménages à trois and even à quatre. Apart from the deep feelings Aton and Enrique have for Tiyi, love is sad, scabrous, and even violent. Do the sexual references reflect the universe you want to describe, a universe where everything rots and decays?

MC Perhaps, yet Enrique's love redeems everything. He is in love with Tiyi, a woman who is not his, who may never be his, who is insane and may never recover her sanity. He is ready to do anything to save her. There is a rather beautiful passion in all of this. Aton himself adores his wife, with whom he no longer has anything in common sexually. It seems to me that these are two powerful images of love.

FP But there is Mandjet, who was raped by her father.

MC We have lived with the illusion that these kinds of things didn't happen in our societies. At the appearance of the very good book by Jacques André, *L'inceste focal en Guadeloupe et en Martinique* (Focal incest in Guadeloupe and Martinique), we said to ourselves, "This is not true. It's a White man talking. Now the truth is crystal clear."

FP In *Crossing the Mangrove*, you speak about homosexuality, and you mention lesbianism in *La colonie du nouveau monde*. Aren't both of these topics taboo in West Indian literature?

MC Except for works by writers like René Depestre, West Indian literature is devoid of sex. As Chamoiseau says, Négritude has no libido. As for homosexuality, things are much worse. In *Black Skins, White Masks*, Frantz Fanon stated positively that it didn't exist in Guadeloupe and Martinique. At a 1993 conference on Créolités that took place at the University of Maryland, Professor James Arnold drew people's attention to this uneasiness or hypocrisy.

FP Yes, because in the final analysis the image of the West Indies is one of virile males and heterosexual love under the coconut trees. . . .

MC Yes, but that is also a stereotype. When I was a little girl, there were groups of women whom people discreetly called *zanmi*. They were living together and dressed alike. Only years later did I understand that they were lesbians.

FP In *La colonie du nouveau monde*, the narrator refers a number of times to a social hierarchy based on class and skin color. Enrique likes Black women and has Black mistresses, but he ends up marrying a White woman, Ramona, because in his country this is what men of his rank do. Similar allusions to such color-based social hierarchies are present in all your previous works. Do these color prejudices in the West Indies also exist in Latin America?

MC In Latin America the whole society is based on color, with hatred and fear of Blacks. Everybody thinks he or she is descended from Whites and also from Indians, because it conveys an exotic touch. Blacks are totally removed from the picture. In reading the works of Manuel Zapata de Oliveia, a Black Colombian writer, and in the course of conversations with him, I realized the dimensions of the color problem and the elimination of whatever is African and Negro from Latin American societies.

FP The theme of incest and child molestation found in *La colonie du nouveau monde* is also present in Toni Morrison's *The Bluest Eye*. You told me that you had a great deal of admiration for her. Do you see similarities between her work and yours?

MC I don't know. I don't believe so. However, it is undeniable that the theme of rape was suggested to me by what goes on in the United States. Had I not lived in the States, this theme might not have come to my mind. Since stories of little girls being raped are constantly shown on screens here, this theme imposed itself on me.

FP Toni Morrison just received the Nobel Prize for literature. What do you think about this?

MC She is undoubtedly a great writer, a remarkable stylist. This may appear a bit critical, but I find her very "politically correct." Unlike Alice Walker, she doesn't venture into topics like excision that may displease or irritate people. She doesn't extol homosexuality as Audre Lorde did. She doesn't proclaim extremist political convictions like Angela Davis. She is not violent. In my opinion, she doesn't disturb anybody. She paints her community, the African-American community, with the tested colors of magical realism.

FP What about Maya Angelou, just honored by President Clinton, who entrusted her with writing a poem for his inauguration?

MC Except for *I Know Why the Caged Bird Sings*, which is a classic, I haven't read Maya Angelou's works. But I like her personality, which comes across in TV interviews, for instance. She seems passionate and dynamic. I once saw her sing and dance on television. I like that.

FP In *La colonie du nouveau monde* and *I, Tituba, Black Witch of Salem*, you describe the intolerance and the fanaticism of crowds, who hasten to condemn Mesketet, one of Aton's disciples, because they need someone to accuse. Is this a new facet of your continual struggle against injustice and errors by the police? Is this a new example of your incredulity concerning man's arbitrary justice? Isn't Mesketet unjustly condemned more for his different religion and lifestyle than for his alleged crime?

MC Jesus Christ was the first one to say that man's justice was imperfect. Remember what the Bible says, "He that is without sin among you, let him cast the first stone. . . ." If we look at what is happening around us, it is true that people don't show any pity for those who are different, who don't cast themselves in a familiar mold. Any difference presents a danger.

FP At one point, Enrique observes the degradation of young drug addicts and the wrongdoings of the police. The narrator of the book comments on Enrique's thoughts and says, "No, better days were not in sight! The condition of the world was worsening, and the end of ideologies was not going to cure its illnesses" [199]. Is this your viewpoint?

MC Throughout the book, Enrique is the author's mouthpiece. Like the author, he was a Marxist. He is still capable of love since he is desperately in love with Tiyi. Enrique does good deeds for Meritaton and helps her leave for Guadeloupe. He is a common type of person in my circles: people who believed in things and who unfortunately no longer believe in anything, or at least not in much, but who maintain an indomitable humaneness.

FP And how do you now envision the world to come?

MC Everybody wonders. Nobody knows the answer to your question. Everybody is waiting, but exactly what are they waiting for? This is precisely the case with Enrique. He does what his conscience tells him to do. He tells his father-in-law that he has to remain a Don Quixote until the end of his life. Yet he no longer believes in what he does.

FP Thus there is no way out. You pose problematic questions concerning a drifting world, but you don't offer any solution.

MC As I already said, the role of the novelist is not to provide solutions. Novelists are here to describe things the way they believe things are. Then it is up to the reader to find answers.

FP So a novelist is an agitator?

MC More a reflection, as Flaubert said. Novelists show what happens, reflect on it, and hope that their reflections will generate a spark.

FP What do you wish for the world at the start of this new year?

MC Don't you think it would be arrogant to formulate wishes for the world? Let presidents of republics do that!

FP In the regional French newspaper *La Dépêche du Midi* of August 22, 1993, Marie-Louise Roubaud wrote about you, "She is our Nadine Gordimer and our Doris Lessing and we don't know it." What do you think of such comparisons?

MC They're quite flattering. A bit overwhelming.

FP You've just returned from Prague. Is West Indian literature known there?

MC Not at all. A few bookstores still carry some old translations of Aimé

138

Césaire's works. Patrick Chamoiseau's *Texaco* was translated, thanks to Milan Kundera. *Tree of Life* may be translated into Czech, thanks to Jarmila Ortova, a literary critic. That's all.

FP What has your stay in Prague brought you?

MC I was impressed. First, I learned a lot about literary plurality. A German-speaking writer like Kafka and a Czech-speaking writer like Kundera peacefully coexist in the same culture. Everything was bathed in a musical atmosphere when I was there. I came back with the whole collection of recordings of the works of Dvořák, of whom I knew only the *New World* Symphony. At the same time, people were relaxed, drinking torrents of Pilsner Urquell beer, a beer I had had in Guinea in the heyday of the Marxist revolution. . . . I realized that I had been obsessed with French culture, which represented Europe for me. . . .

FP And here are my three last questions. First, if you were to look back at your life or career, what would you regret not having accomplished?

MC I don't draw balance sheets. What's the purpose? People do perhaps draw up a balance when they are finished writing, but I am still in the process of writing. I would have to look at what I am doing and distance myself from it, as if my endeavors were over. This is not the case now.

FP My second question: what in your life or career are you the proudest of?

MC What can I be proud of? Maybe I am proud of my granddaughter Raki, whom I consider very beautiful and quite accomplished.

FP And my final question: what is the most intense moment you've experienced in the course of your life?

MC One of the most intense moments of my life was perhaps hurricane Hugo, which swept down on Guadeloupe in 1989. I had heard about hurricanes. My mother had talked to me about the hurricane of 1928, but I had never gone through anything like Hugo. It was a staggering experience.

FP Did such a hurricane look like an apocalypse? Did it evoke for you the finality of the world, the finality of life?

MC No, I simply became extremely frightened. I didn't know when it was going to end. Although frightful, it was at the same time beautiful. All the trees around us were completely destroyed. Wind. Rain. It's at such moments that you fully realize the vulnerability of human beings confronting nature.

Bibliography

WORKS BY MARYSE CONDE
Novels

1995   *La migration des coeurs.* Paris: Robert Laffont.
1993   *La colonie du nouveau monde.* Paris: Robert Laffont.
1992   *Les derniers rois mages.* Paris: Mercure de France.
1989   *Traversée de la Mangrove.* Paris: Mercure de France. Published in English as *Crossing the Mangrove,* trans. Richard Philcox. New York: Doubleday, 1995.
1987   *La vie scélérate.* Paris: Seghers. Published in English as *Tree of Life,* trans. Victoria Reiter. New York: Ballantine, 1992.
1986   *Moi, Tituba, sorcière . . . Noire de Salem.* Paris: Mercure de France. Published in English as *I, Tituba, Black Witch of Salem,* trans. Richard Philcox. Charlottesville: University Press of Virginia, 1992.
1985   *Ségou – La terre en miettes.* Paris: Robert Laffont. Published in English as *The Children of Segu,* trans. Linda Coverdale. New York: Viking Penguin, 1989; New York: Ballantine, 1990.
1984   *Ségou – Les murailles de terre.* Paris: Robert Laffont. Published

in English as *Segu*, trans. Barbara Bray. New York: Viking Penguin, 1987; New York: Ballantine, 1988.

1981 *Une saison à Rihata.* Paris: Robert Laffont. Published in English as *A Season in Rihata*, trans. Richard Philcox. London: Heinemann, 1988.

1976 *Hérémakhonon.* Paris: Union Générale d'Editions. Reprinted as *En attendant le bonheur (Hérémakhonon).* Paris: Seghers, 1988. Published in English as *Heremakhonon*, trans. Richard Philcox. Washington DC: Three Continents Press, 1982.

Plays

1991 "Le morne de Massabielle." Unpublished in French. Published in English as *The Hills of Massabielle*, trans. Richard Philcox. New York: Ubu Repertory Theater Publications.

1989 *An Tan Revolisyon: Elle court, elle court la liberté.* Guadeloupe: Conseil Régional.
"Comédie d'amour." Unpublished; revision, 1992.

1988 *Pension Les Alizés.* Paris: Mercure de France. Published in English as *The Tropical Breeze Hotel*, trans. Barbara Brewster Lewis and Catherine Temerson. In *Plays by Women: An International Anthology*, Book 2. New York: Ubu Repertory Theater Publications, 1994.

1986 "Les sept voyages de Ti-Noël." Unpublished.

1973 *Mort d'Oluwémi d'Ajumako.* Paris: Pierre-Jean Oswald.

1972 *Dieu nous l'a donné.* Paris: Pierre-Jean Oswald.

Short Stories

1991 "No Woman, No Cry." *Le Serpent à plumes*, 3d quarter. Rpt. in *Femmes du monde.* Paris: Le Serpent à Plumes, 1995.

1988 "La châtaigne et le fruit à pain." In Adine Sagalyn, ed., *Voies de pères, voix de filles: Quinze femmes écrivains parlent de leurs pères.* Paris: Maren Sell. Published in English as "The Breadnut and the Breadfruit," trans. Richard Philcox. *Callaloo* 12, no.38 (winter 1989): 134–51.

1985 *Pays-mêlé.* Paris: Hatier.

1984 "Ayissé." In Jacqueline Leiner, ed., *Soleil éclaté: Mélanges offerts à Aimé Césaire à l'occasion de son soixante-dixième anniversaire*. Tubingen: G. Narr.

1982 "Trois femmes à Manhattan." *Présence Africaine*, no.121–22 (1st & 2d quarter): 307–15. Published in English as "Three Women in Manhattan," trans. Thomas Spear. In Lizabeth Paravisini Gebert and Carmen Esteves, eds., *Green Cane and Juices Flotsam*. New Brunswick NJ: Rutgers University Press, 1991.

Children's Literature

1991 *Haiti chérie*. Paris: Bayard.
1990 *Hugo le terrible*. Paris: Sépia.
1989 "Victor et les barricades." *Je Bouquine*, no.61 (March): 13–64.

Other Books

1995 Condé, Maryse, and Madeleine Cottenet-Hage, eds. *Penser la créolité*. Paris: Karthala.
1992 Condé, Maryse, Delphine Perret, Michael Lucey, and Ann Smock, eds. *L'Héritage de Caliban*. Guadeloupe: Editions Jasor.
1988 *Guadeloupe*. Paris: Vilo/Richer, Hoa Qui.
1980 *Tim tim! Bois sec! Bloemlezing uit de Franstalige Caribische Literatuur*. Haarlem: In de Knipscheer.
1979 *La parole des femmes – Essai sur des romancières des Antilles de langue française*. Paris: L'Harmattan.
1978 *Cahier d'un retour au pays natal – Césaire*. Paris: Hatier.
La civilisation du Bossale – Réflexions sur la littérature orale de la Guadeloupe et de la Martinique. Paris: L'Harmattan.
1977 *La poésie antillaise*. Paris: Fernand Nathan.
Le roman antillais. 2 vols. Paris: Fernand Nathan.

Articles

1995 "Chercher nos vérités." In Maryse Condé and Madeleine Cottenet-Hage, eds., *Penser la créolité*. Paris: Karthala.
"Finding Our Voice." *Essence*, May, 193–96.
Foreword (*Avant-propos*) to Valérie Budig-Markin and James Gaasch, eds., *Diversité: La nouvelle francophone à travers le*

monde: Intermediate Reader & Francophone Anthology. Boston: Houghton Mifflin.

"Language and Power: Words as Miraculous Weapons." CLA Journal 39, no.1 (September): 18–25.

1993 "Order, Disorder, Freedom and the West Indian Writer." Yale French Studies 2, no.83: 121–35.

"The Role of the Writer." World Literature Today 67, no.4 (autumn): 697–99.

1992 "Epilogue: Cinema, Literature and Freedom." In Mbye B. Cham, ed., Ex-îles – Essays on Caribbean Cinema. Trenton NJ: Africa World Press.

"J'habite Montebello." Iles, December, 26–27.

"L'île aux femmes." Elite Madame, no.20 (October–November): 14–18.

"Mon grand-père de Guadeloupe." Notre temps, November, 89–90.

1989 "Habiter ce pays, la Guadeloupe." Chemins critiques 1, no.3 (December): 5–14.

"Petit pays au miroir." Globe, no.42 (November): 7 (special section, "La memoire de Hugo").

1988 "Maryse Condé." In Marcel Bisiaux and Catherine Jajolet, eds., Soixante écrivains parlent de leurs mères. Paris: Pierre Horay.

1987 "Notes sur un retour au pays natal." Conjonctions: Revue Franco-Haitienne, no.176, supplement: 6–23.

"Un papillon qui bat de l'aile." Géo Magazine, no.106 (December): 104–8.

1985 "Au-delà des langues et des couleurs." La Quinzaine littéraire 436 (16 March): 36. Published in English as "Beyond Languages and Color," trans. John Williams. Discourse: Journal for Theoretical Studies in Media and Culture 11, no.2 (spring–summer 1989): 109–13.

1984 "Afrique: Mon beau mythe: Entretien avec Guy Tirolien." Notre Librairie, no.74: 26–27.

1983 "In Memoriam – Okot p'Bitek: Hommage et témoignage." Recherche, Pédagogie & Culture, no.63: 71–74, in collaboration with K. Muhindi.

"Naipaul et les Antilles – Une histoire d'amour?" La Quinzaine littéraire, no.403 (16 October): 6–7.

"Parlez-moi d'amour. . . ?" *Autrement*, no.49 (April): 206–12.

1982 "Anglophones et francophones: Les frontières littéraires existent-elles?" *Notre Librairie*, no.65 (July–September): 27–32.

"Entretien avec Lylian Kesteloot." *Recherche, Pédagogie & Culture*, no.57: 85–87.

"La femme antillaise et l'avenir des Antilles françaises." *Croissance des jeunes nations*, no.241 (July–August): 33–35.

"Le vent réveille la pensée des hommes." *Afrique*, no.61 (July): 52.

1981 "Entretien avec Raphaël Ndiaye sur la poésie orale sérèr de la petite côte." *Recherche, Pédagogie & Culture*, no.53–54: 40–42.

"Man, Woman and Love in French Caribbean Writing." *Caribbean Quarterly* 27, no.4 (December): 31–36.

"Sarah Maldoror." *Recherche, Pédagogie & Culture*, no.51: 56–58.

1980 "Claude Vauthier, Hervé Bourges: *Les 50 Afriques*." *Recherche, Pédagogie & Culture*, no.47–48: 54–56.

"Entretien de Maryse Condé avec Tierno Monémembo, auteur de *Les Crapauds-brousse*." *Recherche, Pédagogie & Culture*, no.49: 66–68.

"Entretien de Maryse Condé avec William Sassine." *Recherche, Pédagogie & Culture*, no.49: 64–66.

1979 "L'image de la petite fille dans la littérature féminine des Antilles." *Recherche, Pédagogie & Culture*, no.44: 89–93.

1978 "La création littéraire." In Mohamed Aziza, dir., *Patrimoine culturel et création contemporaine en Afrique et dans le monde arabe*. Dakar/Abidjan: Les Nouvelles Editions Africaines.

"Propos sur l'identité culturelle." In Guy Michaud, ed., *Négritude: Traditions et développement*. Paris: Complexe/PUF.

1976 "La littérature féminine de la Guadeloupe: Recherche d'identité." *Présence Africaine*, no.99–100 (4th quarter): 155–66.

1975 "Civilisation noire de la Diaspora." *Présence Africaine*, no.94 (2d quarter): 184–94.

1974 "Négritude césairienne, Négritude senghorienne." *Revue de littérature comparée* 3, no.4 (July–December): 409–19.

1973 "Batouala." *Présence Africaine*, no.87 (3rd quarter): 212–13 (book review).

"*No Easy Way to Freedom.*" *Présence Africaine*, no.87 (3rd quarter): 215–17 (book review).

"Pourquoi la Négritude? Négritude ou Révolution?" In Jeanne-Lydie Gore, ed., *Négritude africaine, négritude caraïbe*. Paris: Editions de la francité.

"*Proverbes Créoles de la Martinique.*" *Présence Africaine*, no.88 (4th quarter): 232–33 (book review).

"*Les travailleurs étrangers en France.*" *Présence Africaine*, no.88 (4th quarter): 230–32 (book review).

1972 "Autour d'une littérature antillaise." *Présence Africaine*, no.81 (1st quarter): 170–76.

"*Pluie et vent sur Télumée Miracle* de Simone Schwarz-Bart." *Présence Africaine*, no.84 (4th quarter): 138–39.

"Three Female Writers in Modern Africa: Flora Nwapa, Ama Ata Aidoo and Grace Ogot." *Présence Africaine*, no.82 (2d quarter): 132–43.

1971 "La question raciale et la pensée moderne." *Présence Africaine*, no.78 (2d quarter): 240–45.

Translation

Williams, Eric Eustache. *De Christophe Colomb à Fidel Castro: l'Histoire des Caraïbes 1492–1969*, trans. Maryse Condé and Richard Philcox. Paris: Présence Africaine, 1975. Translation of *From Columbus to Castro: The History of the Caribbean 1492–1969*. New York: Harper & Row, 1971.

Writings on Maryse Condé

A., B. and J. S. "Maryse Condé: La Guadeloupe ne m'a pas habituée à tant d'égards." *TV Magazine/France Antilles*, no.285 (1995): 12–13.

Abraham, Marie. "Maryse Condé: 'Il faut perdre la rigidité idéologique.'" *TV Magazine/France Antilles*, no.132 (1992): 21.

Addé, Najet. "Le mystérieux aventurier de Rivière-au-Sel." *Jeune Afrique*, no.1522 (5 March 1990): 65.

Almira, Jacques. "*Moi, Tituba, sorcière noire de Salem.*" *Jours de France*, 25 October 1986, 132.

Andrade, Susan Z. "African Fictions and Feminisms: Making History and Remaking Traditions (Emecheta Buchi, Nwapa Flora, Condé Maryse, Clift Michelle, Ba Mariama, Djebar Assia)." Ph.D. diss., University of Michigan, 1992.

——. "The Nigger of the Narcissist: History, Sexuality and Intertextuality in Maryse Condé's *Heremakhonon*." *Callaloo* 16, no.1 (winter 1993): 213–26.

Andréani, Carole. "La voix du pays natal." *Antoinette*, January 1990, 9.

Antoine, Régis. *La littérature franco-antillaise*. Paris: Karthala, 1992.

Araújo, Nara. "The Contribution of Women's Writing to the Literature and Intellectual Achievements of the Caribbean: *Moi, Tituba, Sorcière* and *Amour, Colère et Folie*." *Journal of Black Studies* 25 (December 1994): 217–30.

Arentsen, Maria Fernanda. "*Moi, Tituba, Sorcière* . . . de Maryse Condé et *La culpa es de los Tlaxcaltecas* d'Elena Garro: Deux expressions féminines du réalisme merveilleux." Master's thesis, Université Laval, 1994.

Arnold, A. James. "The Erotics of Colonialism." *New West Indian Guide* 68, no.1–2 (1994): 5–22.

——. "The Gendering of Créolité." In Maryse Condé and Madeleine Cottenet-Hage, eds., *Penser la créolité*. Paris: Karthala, 1995.

——. "The Novelist as Critic." *World Literature Today* 67, no.4 (autumn 1993): 711–16.

——. "Poétique forcée et identité dans la littérature des Antilles francophones." In Maryse Condé, Delphine Perret, Michael Lucey, and Ann Smock, eds., *L'Héritage de Caliban*. Guadeloupe: Editions Jasor, 1992.

Babin, Céline. "*Moi, Tituba, sorcière* . . . *Noire de Salem*." *Nuit blanche*, no.28 (May–June 1987): 29.

Baldewyns, Claire. "Maryse Condé a du punch citron." *L'Evénement du Jeudi*, 19 April 1990, 111.

Balutansky, Kathleen M. "Creating her own image: Female genesis in *Mémoire d'une amnésique* and *Moi, Tituba, sorcière*." In Maryse Condé, Delphine Perret, Michael Lucey, and Ann Smock, eds., *L'Héritage de Caliban*. Guadeloupe: Editions Jasor, 1992.

——. "Créolité in Question: Caliban in Maryse Condé's *Traversée de la Mangrove*." In Maryse Condé and Madeleine Cottenet-Hage, eds., *Penser la créolité*. Paris: Karthala, 1995.

146

Banaias, Chris. "*Ségou* ou Maryse Condé à la recherche de ses racines." *Afrique Antilles Magazine*, no.63 (July–August 1984): 14.

Barland, Jean-Rémi. "Maryse Condé: La mémoire des Antilles." *Le Provençal*, 12 April 1992, 26.

Baudot, Alain. "Maryse Condé ou la parole du refus." *Recherche, Pédagogie & Culture*, no.57 (April–June 1982): 30–35.

Beaumarchais, Jean-Pierre de. *Dictionnaire des littératures de langue française* Paris: Bordas, 1984.

Bécel, Pascale. "*Moi, Tituba, sorciére . . . noire de Salem* As a Tale of 'Petite Marronne.'" *Callaloo* 18, no.3 (summer 1995): 608–15.

Berrian, Brenda F. *Bibliography of Women Writers from the Caribbean: 1831–1986*. Washington DC: Three Continents Press, 1989.

——. "Masculine Roles and Triangular Relationships in Maryse Condé's *Une saison à Rihata.*" *Bridges: A Senegalese Journal of English Studies/Revue Sénégalaise d'Etudes Anglaises*, vol.3 (1991): 5–20.

Blardone, Gilbert. "La femme antillaise et l'avenir des Antilles françaises," *Croissance des jeunes nations*, July–August 1982, 33–35.

Blundell, Janet Boyarin. "Condé Maryse. *Segu.*" *Library Journal*, vol.112 (1 March 1987): 91.

Boiro, Gaëtane. "Avec Maryse Condé, découvrez la sorcière de Salem mais aussi . . . des émouvantes révélations sur la société américaine." *Afrique Antilles Magazine*, no.84 (October–November 1986): 12–13.

——. "Maryse Condé – Mon objectif: Aider l'identité antillaise à s'affirmer." *Afrique Antilles*, October 1985, 13.

Boisriveaud, Juliette. "*Traversée de la Mangrove.*" *Cosmopolitan* (France), April 1990, 55.

Bouraoui, Hédi. "Maryse Condé." *Ecriture française dans le monde*, no.5 (May 1981): 67–71.

Bovoso, Carole. "*Heremakhonon.*" *Essence*, no.13 (April 1983): 19.

Brierre, Jean F. "L'art de faire vivre l'histoire." *Afrique nouvelle*, no.1858 (13 February 1985): 14.

Browne, Phiefer L. "Maryse Condé. *Segu.*" *Black American Literature Forum* 23, no.1 (spring 1989): 183–85.

Bruner, Charlotte H. "*Entretiens avec Maryse Condé . . . .*" *World Literature Today* 68, no.4 (autumn 1994): 863–64.

——. "*Moi, Tituba, sorcière . . . noire de Salem.*" *World Literature Today* 61, no.2 (spring 1987): 337–38.

Bruner, Charlotte, and David Bruner. "Buchi Emecheta and Maryse Condé: Contemporary Writing from Africa and the Caribbean." *World Literature Today* 59, no.1 (winter 1985): 9–13.

Bruner, David K. "Maryse Condé: Creative Writer in a Political World." *L'Esprit Créateur* 12, no.2 (summer 1977): 168–73.

——. "Maryse Condé. *Hérémakhonon.*" *World Literature Today* 51, no.3 (summer 1977): 494.

——. "Maryse Condé's *Ségou 2: La terre en miettes.*" *World Literature Today* 60, no.3 (summer 1986): 509.

——. "*Une saison à Rihata.*" *World Literature Today* 56, no.2 (spring 1982): 390–91.

——. "*La vie scélérate.*" *World Literature Today* 62, no.3 (summer 1988): 498.

Busby, Margaret, ed. *Daughters of Africa.* New York: Pantheon Books, 1992.

C., A. "*Traversée de la Mangrove.*" *Femme d'aujourd'hui,* 1 February 1990, 32.

C., C. "Chasse à la sorcière." *Impact médecin,* 4 April 1987, 17.

Canneval, Jacques. "Maryse Condé invite les hommes au dialogue." *Le Matin,* 3 November 1986, 19.

Carnavaggio, Pierre. "Trois femmes de leur temps." *Panorama du Médecin,* no.3135 (13 March 1990): 48–49.

Casanova, Nicole. "Touche pas à la femme noire." *Le Quotidien de Paris,* 3 February 1987, 18.

Chaillot, Nicole. "Enfances . . . ." *L'Unité,* no.667 (17 November 1986): 29.

Chamoiseau, Patrick. "Reflections on Maryse Condé's *Traversée de la Mangrove.*" *Callaloo* 14, no.2 (spring 1991): 389–95.

Chevrier, Jacques. "Ecriture noire en question." *Notre Librairie,* no.65 (July–September 1982): 7–16.

——. "La malédiction des Traoré." *Jeune Afrique,* no.1311 (19 February 1986): 62–63.

——. "Maryse Condé, la grande éclectique." *Jeune Afrique,* no.1706 (16 September 1993): 68–69.

——. "Une patrie mythique." *Jeune Afrique,* no.1088 (11 November 1981): 94.

——. "Sur les traces des Bambaras." *Jeune Afrique,* no.1223 (13 June 1984): 64–65.

——. "Voyage au centre de la mémoire." *Jeune Afrique*, no.1659 (22 October 1992): 45.

Chikha, Elizabeth. "La saga d'une famille guadeloupéenne de Marcus Garvey à Sékou Touré. Les fruits de *Ségou*." *Jeune Afrique*, no.1405 (9 December 1987): 51.

"*The Children of Segu* by Maryse Condé." *American Visions* 6, no.1 (February 1991): 38.

Chinosole. "Maryse Condé as Contemporary Griot in *Segu*." *Callaloo* 18, no.3 (summer 1995): 593–601.

Clark, Vèvè A. "Developing Diaspora Literacy: Allusion in Maryse Condé's *Hérémakhonon*." In Carole Boyce Davies and Elaine Savory Fido, eds., *Out of the Kumbla: Caribbean Women and Literature*. Trenton NJ: Africa World Press, 1990.

——. "Developing Diaspora Literacy and 'Marasa' Consciousness." In Hortense J. Spillers, ed., *Comparative American Identities: Race, Sex and Nationality in the Modern Text*. New York: Routledge Publishers, 1991.

——. "Je me suis réconciliée avec mon île." *Callaloo* 12, no.1 (winter 1989): 85–132.

Clavel, Andre. "Writers Without Borders." *World Press Review* 40, no.12 (December 1993): 49.

Clément, Marie-Gabrielle. "Dans la vitrine du libraire." *Femme d'aujourd'hui*, 13 January 1988, 20.

Colby, Vineta, ed. *World Authors 1980–1985*. New York: H. W. Wilson, 1991.

Colonna-Césari, Annick. "Les derniers rois mages." *L'Express International*, no.2139 (10 July 1992): 63.

——. "L'esclave couronné – La quête d'identité d'une famille guadeloupéenne hantée par l'ancêtre africain." *L'Express*, 2 July 1992, 97.

Comberousse, Françoise de. "Seule la mort l'a délivrée de sa seconde naissance." *France-Soir*, 8 October 1986, 19.

——. "Tituba fait beaucoup pour le bonheur de Maryse Condé et de Simone Gallimard." *France-Soir*, 21 March 1987, 11.

"Condé, Maryse. *The Children of Segu*." *Kirkus Reviews* 57, no.16 (1 September 1989): 1267.

"Condé, Maryse. *I, Tituba, Black Witch of Salem*." *Kirkus Reviews* 60, no.13 (1 July 1992): 795.

"Condé, Maryse. *Segu*." *Kirkus Reviews* 55, no.1 (1 January 1987): 4–5.

"Condé, Maryse. *Tree of Life*." *Kirkus Reviews* 60, no.13 (1 July 1992): 795.

Constant, Denis. "L'Afrique à Distance." *L'Humanité*, 4 March 1985, 11.

——. "Les pays mêlés de Maryse Condé." *L'Humanité Dimanche*, 28 February 1986, 38.

——. "*Ségou.*" *L'Humanité Dimanche*, 10 August 1984, 9.

Coppermann, Annie. "*Ségou.*" *Les échos*, 15 June 1984, 21.

Cornevin, Robert. "Maryse Condé, *Moi, Tituba, sorcière noire de Salem.*" *Mondes et Cultures*, 29 July 1987, 608.

Couffon, Claude. "Au coeur de la terre antillaise." *Magazine littéraire*, no.276 (April 1990): 57.

——. "Maryse Condé: *Traversée de la Mangrove.*" *Magazine litteraire*, no.276 (April 1990): 57.

Crequé-Harris, Leah. "Literature of the Diaspora by Women of Color." *Sage* 3, no.2 (fall 1986): 61–64.

Crosta, Suzanne. "Narrative and Discursive Strategies in Maryse Condé's *Traversée de la Mangrove.*" *Callaloo* 15, no.1 (winter 1992): 147–55.

d'Argon, Benoîte. "Maryse Condé entre Amériques et Francophonie." *TV Magazine/France-Antilles*, no.176 (1993): 11–13.

——. "Qu'est-ce qu'elle écrit déjà?" *TV Magazine/France-Antilles*, no.285 (1995): 13–14.

Darnal, Antoine et al. "Maryse Condé." *Notre Librairie*, no.108 (January–March 1992): 157–58, 170.

Davies, Carole Boyce, and Elaine Savory Fido, eds. *Out of the Kumbla: Caribbean Women and Literature*. Trenton NJ: Africa World Press, 1992.

Davis, Angela Y. Foreword to Maryse Condé, *I, Tituba, Black Witch of Salem*, trans. Richard Philcox. Charlottesville: University Press of Virginia, 1992.

Deberre, Jean-Christophe. "*Ségou, les murailles de terre.*" *Notre Librairie*, no.75–76 (July–October 1984): 226–28.

Degras, Priska. "Maryse Condé: d'Afriques en Amériques." *Notre Librairie*, no.104 (January–March 1991): 72–75.

——. "Maryse Condé: L'ecriture de l'histoire," *L'Esprit Créateur* 33, no.2 (summer 1993): 73–81.

——. "Maryse Condé, *Pays mêlé.*" *Notre Librairie*, no.111 (October–December 1992): 139.

Delannoy, Stéphane. "Maryse Condé ou le retour au roman." *TV Magazine/France-Antilles*, no.12 (16 December 1989): 37–40.

Démeron, Pierre. "La noire qui n'a pas besoin de nègre." *Marie-Claire*, December 1987, 287–89.

DeSouza, Pascale. "Inscription du créole dans les textes francophones." In Maryse Condé and Madeleine Cottenet-Hage, eds., *Penser la créolité*. Paris: Karthala, 1995.

Dieckmann, Katherine. "Magic Wan – *Tree of Life* by Maryse Condé, *Curfew* by Jose Donoso, *Maqroll: Three Novellas* by Alvaro Mutis and Others," *Village Voice* 39, no.23 (7 June 1994): SS30.

Dommergues, Pierre. "Etre esclave à la Barbade." *Le Monde Diplomatique*, March 1987, 26.

Dorsinville, Roger. "Maryse la bambara." *Africa*, no.162 (June 1984): 90.

——. "*Une saison à Rihata.*" *Africa*, November 1981, 95–96.

Dukats, Mara L. "Antillean Challenges to Universalism: Narrativizing the Diverse: A Study of Selected Works by Patrick Chamoiseau, Maryse Condé, Edouard Glissant, and Daniel Maximin." Ph.D. diss., Northwestern University, 1993.

——. "The Hybrid Terrain of Literary Imagination: Maryse Condé's Black Witch of Salem, Nathaniel Hawthorne's Hester Prynne, and Aimé Césaire's Heroic Poetic Voice," *College Literature* 22, no.1 (February 1995): 51–61.

——. "A Narrative of Violated Maternity: *Moi, Tituba, sorcière . . . Noire de Salem.*" *World Literature Today* 67, no.4 (autumn 1993): 745–50.

Eibel, Alfred. "*Traversée de la Mangrove.*" *Africa*, April 1990, 97.

F., C. "*Les derniers rois mages.*" *Lire*, April 1992, 103.

F., G. "Maryse Condé: La rêve dans le lit de la réalité." *France-Antilles*, 22 December 1989, 4.

Fabre, Marie. "*Moi, Tituba, sorcière noire de Salem* par Maryse Condé." *Croissance des jeunes nations*, no.293 (April 1987): 45.

Fisher, Stephen H. "Ripped from Africa's Breast." *Newsday*, 24 December 1989, 23 (Ideas section).

Fister, Barbara. "For Our Silent Sisters: Third World Women's Literature." *Choice* 29, no.1 (September 1991): 39–47.

Flannigan, Arthur. "Reading Below the Belt: Sex and Sexuality in Françoise Ega and Maryse Condé." *French Review* 62, no.2 (December 1988): 300–312.

Flor, Paola. "*Moi, Tituba, sorcière noire de Salem.*" *Afrique-Asie*, 26 January 1987, 52.

Fonkoua, Romuald. "Panorama de la nouvelle antillaise." *Notre Librairie*, no.111 (October–December 1992): 68–82.

Franck, Sarah. "*Traversée de la Mangrove.*" *Télérama*, no.2098 (28 March 1990): 17.

Franck, Sophie. "La plume au féminin." *Soir illustré*, 12 May 1988, 94–95.

Fratta, Carla. "Entrevue avec Maryse Condé, écrivain guadeloupéen." *Caribana*, vol.1 (1990): 85–92.

Frebourg, Olivier. "*Traversée de la Mangrove.*" *Le Figaro*, 29 January 1990, 18.

Frey, Pascale. "*Ségou*: Une grande saga africaine." *Tribune de Gevève*, 21 June 1984, 3.

G., S. "L'histoire romancée: Maryse Condé et la sorcière." *La Suisse*, 2 March 1987, 11.

Galanti, Marie. "De la culture à la politique: Maryse Condé s'engage." *Journal français d'Amérique*, 11 April 1986, 10–11.

García, Cristina. "The Rich Cadence of Caribbean Life as Conveyed by Novelist Maryse Condé." *Chicago Tribune*, 11 October 1992, 6 (section 14).

Garcin, Jérome. "*Une saison à Rihata.*" *Les Nouvelles littéraires*, no.2808 (15 October 1981): 33.

Gassa, Néjib. "Maryse Condé: 'La réussite individuelle est un peu une trahison.'" *Réalités*, no.169 (4 November 1988): 40–41.

Gautheyrou, Michelle. "Maryse Condé: Les malheurs d'une sorcière." *Le Figaro littéraire*, 29 December 1986, 6.

——. "Des murailles fragiles." *Le Figaro*, 3 June 1984, 25.

Genevoix, Sylvie. "*Ségou – Les murailles de terre.*" *Madame Figaro*, no.12357 (26 May 1984): 37–39.

George, Bernard. "*Ségou – Les murailles de terre* de Maryse Condé." *Jours de France*, 16 June 1984, 110.

Girard, Isabelle. "Maryse Condé: Je suis pour l'indépendance." *L'Evénement du Jeudi*, no.160 (26 November–2 December 1987): 112–13.

Goldberg, Stephanie. "Maryse Condé Makes Art of Salem's Black Witch." *Chicago Tribune*, 22 September 1992, 3 (section 2).

Goodwin, David. "*The Children of Segu.*" *New York Times Book Review*, 31 December 1989, 13.

Goubin, Jean-Luc. "L'engagement: Maryse Condé descend dans l'arène politique." *Le Griot des Antilles*, no.17 (April–May 1992): 4.

Guillaume, A. J., Jr. "*I, Tituba, Black Witch of Salem*." *Choice* 30, no.5 (January 1993): 802.

Guissard, Lucien. "Les chercheurs d'or." *La Croix*, 15 November 1986, 12.

Hardy, Sarah Boykin. "A Poetics of Immediacy: The Short Story and Oral Narrative Theory (Joyce, James; Faulkner, William; Condé, Maryse . . .)." Ph.D. diss., Princeton University, 1993.

Hazael-Massieux, Guy. "Maryse Condé: Retour au pays natal." *Le Provençal*, 1 April 1990, 27.

Henning, Christophe. "*Les derniers rois mages*." *La Voix du Nord*, 11 June 1992, 19.

Herdeck, Donald E., ed. *Caribbean Writers: A Bio-Bibliographical-Critical Encyclopedia*. Washington DC: Three Continents Press, 1979.

Hermine, Nathalie. "Tous les chemins mènent au livre." *Le Journal de l'île de la Réunion*, 27 September 1989, 2.

Herndon, Crystal Cerise. "Gender Construction and Neocolonialism," *World Literature Today* 67, no.4 (autumn 1993): 731–36.

——. "Gendered Fictions of Self and Community: Autobiography and Autoethnography in Caribbean Women's Writing (Schwarz-Bart, Simone; Rhys, Jean; Condé, Maryse; Kincaid, Jamaica . . .)." Ph.D. diss., University of Texas, Austin, 1994.

Hewitt, Leah D. "Condé's Critical Seesaw." *Callaloo* 18, no.3 (summer 1995): 641–51.

——. "Inventing Antillean Narrative: Maryse Condé and Literary Tradition." *Studies in Twentieth Century Literature* 17, no.1 (winter 1993): 79–96.

——. "Mediations of Identity through the Atlantic Triangle: Maryse Condé's *Heremakhonon*." In Leah D. Hewitt, *Autobiographical Tightropes*. Lincoln: University of Nebraska Press, 1990.

Houédanou, Lucien. "Les oubliés de l'histoire officielle." *Afrique Nouvelle*, no.1858 (13 February 1985): 15.

Houssin, Monique. "L'éclate ghetto – Un entretien avec la romancière guadeloupéenne Maryse Condé." *L'Humanité Dimanche*, 20 November 1987, 36–37.

——. "Imaginaire Caraïbe – *Les derniers rois mages* de Maryse Condé ou le roman des légendes antillaises." *L'Humanité Dimanche*, no.112 (7 May 1992): 80.

———. "*La Traversée de la Mangrove* de Maryse Condé – Une nuit pour une vie." *L'Humanité Dimanche*, 2 February 1990, 33.

Hutchison, Paul E. "Fiction – *Crossing the Mangrove* by Maryse Conde." *Library Journal* 120, no.5 (15 March 1995): 96.

"*I, Tituba, Black Witch of Salem*." *Chicago Tribune*, 26 December 1993, 2 (Tribune books section).

"*I, Tituba, Black Witch of Salem*." *Publishers Weekly* 239, no.31 (13 July 1992): 45.

Jacquey, Marie-Clotilde. "*Ségou* est-il un roman malien?" *Notre Librairie*, no.84 (July–September 1986): 56–60.

Jacquey, Marie-Clotilde, and Monique Hugon. "L'Afrique, un continent difficile: Entretien avec Maryse Condé." *Notre Librairie*, vol.74 (January–March 1984): 21–25.

Jeay, Anne-Marie. "*Ségou – Les murailles de terre* – Lecture anthropologique d'un roman d'aventure." *Nouvelles du Sud*, vol.4 (May–July 1986): 115–37.

Johnson, Chalis. "*I, Tituba, Black Witch of Salem* by Maryse Condé." *Black Scholar* 24, no.1 (winter 1994): 64.

Johnson, George. "*The Children of Segu*." *New York Times Book Review*, 25 November 1990, 32.

———. "*Segu* by Maryse Condé." *New York Times Book Review*, 19 June 1988, 32.

Johnson, Lemuel A. "Sisters of Anarcha: Speculum in a New World? Caribbean Literature and a Feminist Hermeneutic." In Stephen H. Arnold, ed., *African Literature Studies: The Present State*. Washington DC: Three Continents Press, 1985.

Julliard, Claire. "Enchanteurs Afro-Créoles." *Dynasteurs*, March 1990, 102–5.

Kadima-Nzugi, Mukala. "Entretien avec Maryse Condé, essayiste et romancière antillaise." *Recherche, Pédagogie & Culture*, vol.28 (1977): 53–54.

Kadir, Djelal. "On Being at the Other End of the World." *World Literature Today* 67, no.4 (autumn 1993): 695–96.

Kaplan, Howard. "*Segu* by Maryse Condé." *Los Angeles Times*, 8 March 1987, 4 (book review section).

154

Kavaliunas, Jolita. "Pénombre et clair-obscur dans la *Traversée de la Mangrove* de Maryse Condé." *Francographies* 2, special issue (1993): 31–39.

Kendall, Elaine. "Tales of the French West Indies . . . *Tree of Life; I, Tituba Black Witch of Salem*." *Los Angeles Times*, 3 January 1993, 3 (book review section).

Kent, Bill. "A Second Chapter in an African Saga," *Philadelphia Inquirer*, 12 November 1989, 4F.

King, Adele. "Two Caribbean Women Go to Africa: Maryse Condé's *Hérémakhonon* and Myriam Warner-Vieyra's *Juletane*." *College Literature* 18, no.3 (October 1991): 96–105.

Knutson, April Ann. "Teaching *Heremakhonon*." *Women in French Newsletter* 8, no.2 (October 1994): 5.

Koch, Kathy. "Storyteller Traces Route of African Culture's Decline." *Christian Science Monitor*, 13 December 1988, 7, 10.

Kormos, Danielle. "A propos de *La Traversée de la Mangrove*." In Maryse Condé, Delphine Perret, Michael Lucey, and Ann Smock, eds., *L'Héritage de Caliban*. Guadeloupe: Editions Jasor, 1992.

Kubayanda, Josaphat. "The Phenomenon of Recognition: The African Ideal in the Caribbean Text." *Journal of Caribbean Studies* 8, no.3 (winter 1991): 175–85.

Lafrenière, Suzanne. "*Moi, Tituba, sorcière noire de Salem* – De l'histoire à la fiction." *Le Droit* (Ottawa-Hull), 14 March 1987, 56.

Lamiot, Christophe. "Maryse Condé, la république des corps." In Maryse Condé and Madeleine Cottenet-Hage, eds., *Penser la créolité*. Paris: Karthala, 1995.

——. "A Question of Questions through a Mangrove Wood (The Literature of Guadeloupe and Martinique)." *Callaloo* 15, no.1 (winter 1992): 138–48.

Laplagne, Geneviève. "Tituba, la sorcière oubliée de Salem." *La Vie*, no.2145 (8 October 1986), 18–19.

——. "*Traversée de Mangrove* [sic]." *Famille Chrétienne*, 15 March 1990, 84–85.

Lara, Hor-Fari. "Un nouveau Condé: *La colonie du nouveau monde*." *Le Flamboyant des Caraïbes*, October 1993, 9.

Larson, Charles R. "Converts and Concubines: *Segu*." *New York Times Book Review*, 31 May 1987, 47.

———. "A Song of Praise for Africa – *The Children of Segu*." *Washington Post*, 8 December 1989, C3.

Leclercq, Pierre-Robert. "Le Tim Tim de Maryse Condé." *Le Monde*, 24 April 1992, 27.

Lefort, Bernard. "Romancière de la mémoire." *Femme d'aujourd'hui*, 26 February 1990, 8–9.

Lemire, Laurent. "Maryse Condé, le style créole." *La Croix*, 8 February 1990, 24.

Lenk, Cynthia Ruth. "Race, Gender, and Personal Power in Selected Contemporary Caribbean Works of Fiction." Ph.D. diss., University of Arkansas, 1990.

Lewis, Barbara. "No Silence: An Interview with Maryse Condé." *Callaloo* 18, no.3 (summer 1995): 543–50.

Lewis, Sandra. "La condition de la femme dans les oeuvres de Maryse Condé." Master's thesis, Ottawa, Bibliothèque Nationale du Canada, 1984.

Lewis, Tess Doering. "*I, Tituba* Subverts History and Infuses a Tale with Spirit." *Boston Sunday Globe*, 20 September 1992, B44.

Lionnet, Françoise. "Happiness Deferred: Maryse Condé's *Heremakhonon* and the Failure of Enunciation." In Françoise Lionnet, *Autobiographical Voices: Race, Gender, Self-Portraiture*. Ithaca: Cornell University Press, 1989.

———. "Savoir du corps et écritures de l'exil: Les romancières de la diaspora antillaise et le mythe de l'authenticité." In Maryse Condé, Delphine Perret, Michael Lucey, and Ann Smock, eds., *L'Héritage de Caliban*. Guadeloupe: Editions Jasor, 1992.

———. "*Traversée de la Mangrove* de Maryse Condé: Vers un nouvel humanisme antillais?" *French Review* 66, no.3 (February 1993): 475–86.

Loncke, Joycelynne. "The Image of the Woman in Caribbean Literature: With Special Reference to *Pan Beat* and *Heremakhonon*." *Bim* 16, no.64 (December 1978): 272–81.

Lucey, Michael. "Voices Accounting for the Past: Maryse Condé's *Traversée de la Mangrove*." In Maryse Condé, Delphine Perret, Michael Lucey, and Ann Smock, eds., *L'Héritage de Caliban*. Guadeloupe: Editions Jasor, 1992.

M., B. "Racines errantes." *Mot pour Mot*, no.16 (October 1984): 77–79.

M., C. "Maryse Condé, *Moi, Tituba, sorcière*." *Marie-Claire*, October 1986, 410.

156

M., J. "Une Guadeloupe inattendue." *La Marseillaise,* 4 February 1990, 7.

M., J.-B. "*Moi, Tituba, sorcière . . .* par Maryse Condé." *L'Express,* 10 October 1986, 160.

Magnier, Bernard. "Les blessures de l'histoire." *La Quinzaine littéraire,* no.455 (16–31 January 1986): 16–17.

——. "Les goûts de Maryse." *Africa international,* no.213, February 1989, 65.

——. "*Traversée de la Mangrove* de Maryse Condé." *Le Mauricien,* 20 April 1990, 8.

——. "*Traversée de la Mangrove* de Maryse Condé: Retour au pays." *Al-maghrib,* 5 April 1990, 16.

——. "*Traversée de la Mangrove* de Maryse Condé: Le retour au pays natal." *L'Opinion,* 18 March 1990, 8.

Makward, Christiane P. "Reading Maryse Condé's Theater." *Callaloo* 18, no. 3 (summer 1995): 681–89.

Makward, Christiane, and Odile Cazenave. "The Others' Others: Francophone Women and Writing." *Yale French Studies,* no.75 (1988): 190–207.

Manzor-Coats, Lillian. "Of Witches and Other Things: Maryse Condé's Challenges to Feminist Discourse." *World Literature Today* 67, no.4 (autumn 1993): 737–44.

Marchand, Valérie. "Enquête sur un roi." *La Croix,* 3–4 May 1992, 15.

Martinez, Josepha. "Avec *Les derniers rois mages,* Maryse Condé nous entraîne aux Antilles et aux Étas-Unis sur les traces de Djeré, Justin, Spéro, descendants d'un roi africain et hantés par leur histoire." *La Marseillaise Dimanche,* 5 April 1992, 5.

Mazingarbe, Danièle. "*Moi, Tituba, sorcière noire de Salem.*" *Figaro Madame,* 28 February 1987, 31.

——. "*Traversée de la Mangrove.*" *Madame Figaro,* 20 January 1990, 25.

McAteer, M. J. "*I, Tituba, Black Witch of Salem.*" *Washington Post Book World,* 6 September 1992, 9.

McCallister, Myrna J. "*Heremakhonon.*" *Library Journal* 107, no.10 (15 May 1982): 1009.

Mekel, Alexyna. "Maryse Condé: Écrivain antillais." *Caribbean Contact,* December 1987, 11.

Mekkawi, Mohamed. *Maryse Condé: Novelist, Playwright, Critic,*

Teacher: An Introductory Biobibliography. Washington DC: Howard University Libraries, 1990.

Merand, Patrick. "Qui êtes-vous . . . Maryse Condé?" *Sépia,* 1st quarter 1990, 5–8.

Meudal, Gérard. "Elles et les îles." *Libération,* 15–16 November 1986, 30–31.

———. "La mystère de l'île à ragots." *Libération,* 18 January 1990, 24.

———. "Si Maryse m'était Condé." *Libération,* 31 December 1985, 23.

Midiohouan, Guy Ossito. "Maryse Condé: *Ségou, les murailles de terre.*" *Peuples noirs, peuples africains,* no.40 (July–August 1984): 81–84.

Mobailly, Dominique. "Maryse Condé met en scène la Guadeloupe – *La traversée de la Mangrove.*" *La Vie,* no.2321 (22 February 1990): 32.

Mordecai, Pamela, and Betty Wilson, eds. *Her True True Name.* Portsmouth NH: Heinemann Educational Books, 1989.

Morrison, Anthea. "Emancipating the Voice: Maryse Condé's *La vie scélérate.*" *Callaloo* 18, no.3 (summer 1995): 616–25.

Mortimer, Mildred. "A Sense of Place and Space in Maryse Condé's *Les derniers rois mages.*" *World Literature Today* 67, no.4 (autumn 1993): 757–62.

Mosher, Howard Frank. "Staying Alive." *New York Times Book Review,* 25 October 1992, 11–12.

Moudileno, Lydie. "Ecrire l'écrivain: Créolité et spécularité." In Maryse Condé and Madeleine Cottenet-Hage, eds., *Penser la créolité.* Paris: Karthala, 1995.

———. "Portrait of the Artist as Dreamer: Maryse Condé's *Traversée de la Mangrove* and *Les derniers rois mages.*" *Callaloo* 18, no.3 (summer 1995): 626–40.

Moulaye, Zeïni. "*Une saison à Rihata* de Maryse Condé." *Présence Africaine,* no.121–22 (1st quarter 1982): 426–28.

Mouralis, Bernard. "*Une saison à Rihata* ou le thriller immobile." *Nouvelles du Sud,* vol.3 (February–April 1986): 23–29.

Mudimbé-Boyi, Elisabeth. "Giving a Voice to Tituba: The Death of the Author?" *World Literature Today* 67, no.4 (autumn 1993): 751–56.

Muhindi, K. "*Hérémakhonon* de Maryse Condé." *Présence Africaine,* no.124 (4th quarter 1982): 239–41.

Mukamabano, Madeleine. "Maryse Condé: 'Tous les peuples noirs de la terre ont un droit de regard sur l'Afrique.'" *Actuel Développement*, September–October 1984, 52–53.

Munley, Ellen W. "Mapping the Mangrove: Empathy and Survival in *Traversée de la Mangrove*." *Callaloo* 15, no.1 (winter 1992): 156–66.

Murdoch, H. Adlai. "Divided Desire: Biculturality and the Representation of Identity in *En attendant le bonheur*." *Callaloo* 18, no.3 (summer 1995): 579–92.

Mutombo, Kanyana. "Entretien avec . . . Maryse Condé, 'Madame Ségou.'" *Echos Africains*, 1984, 6–8.

Naudin, Marie. "*La vie scélérate*." *French Review* 61, no.6 (May 1988): 987–88.

Needham, George. "*Crossing the Mangrove* by Maryse Condé, translated by Richard Philcox." *Booklist* 91, no.12 (15 February 1995): 1057.

Newman, Miller. "Tied to a Spinner's Shuttle – *Tree of Life* by Maryse Condé, translated by Victoria Reiter; *I, Tituba, Black Witch of Salem* by Maryse Condé, translated by Richard Philcox. . . ." *Belles Lettres* 9, no.3 (spring 1994): 48, 52.

Ngandu Nkashama, Pius. "L'Afrique en pointillé dans *Une saison à Rihata* de Maryse Condé." *Notre Librairie*, vol.73 (1984): 31–37.

Ngate, Jonathan. "Maryse Condé and Africa: The Making of a Recalcitrant Daughter?" *A Current Bibliography on African Affairs* 19, no.1 (1986–87): 5–20.

Nicoloni, Elisabeth. "*Les derniers rois mages*." *La Vie*, no.2441 (11 June 1992): 54.

——. "Un entretien avec Maryse Condé – La sorcière noire de Salem." *Jeune Afrique*, no.1345 (15 October 1986): 76–79.

——. "Maryse, la sorcière bien aimée." *Jeune Afrique*, no.1368 (25 March 1987): 20.

Nyatetu-Waigwa, Wangari wa. "From Liminality to a Home of Her Own? The Quest Motif in Maryse Condé's Fiction." *Callaloo* 18, no.3 (summer 1995): 551–64.

Obejas, Achy. "The Part of Paradise You Won't See in the Travel Posters." *Los Angeles Times*, 21 August 1995, E4.

Obradovic, Nadezda. "Maryse Condé. *Les derniers rois mages*." *World Literature Today* 66, no.3 (summer 1992): 564.

Okpanachi, Sunday. "L'Antillais en Afrique: du mirage à l'image – Une réflexion sur *Hérémakhonon* de Maryse Condé et *Ti Jean l'Horizon* de

Simone Schwarz-Bart." *Peuples noirs, peuples africains*, no.40 (July–August 1984): 51–63.

———. "*Une saison à Rihata* de Maryse Condé et *Juletane* de Myriam Warner-Vieyra." *Ecriture française dans le monde* 6, no.15–16 (1984): 80–86.

Owomoyela, Oyekan. "Maryse Condé, *Segu*." *Prairie Schooner* 64, no.1 (spring 1990): 127–29.

P., A. M. "Tiraillements." *La Cité*, 28 June 1990, 62.

P., I. "*Les derniers rois mages*." *L'Evénement du Jeudi*, 21 May 1992, 136.

P., Y. "*Moi, Tituba, sorcière noire de Salem*." *Pélerin Magazine*, 9 January 1987, 58.

Pageard, Robert. *Littérature négro-africaine – Le mouvement littéraire contemporain dans l'Afrique noire d'expression française*. 4th ed. Paris: L'Ecole, 1979.

Pagnard, Rose-Marie. "*Moi, Tituba, sorcière . . . noire de Salem*." *Coopération*, no.12 (19 March 1987): 41.

Peroncel-Hugoz, J.-P. "Sous l'arbre du voyageur." *Le Monde*, 19 May 1990, 19.

Perret, Delphine. "Dialogue with the Ancestors." *Callaloo* 18, no.3 (summer 1995): 652–67.

———. "L'Écriture mosaïque de *Traversée de la Mangrove*." In Maryse Condé, Delphine Perret, Michael Lucey, and Ann Smock, eds., *L'Héritage de Caliban*. Guadeloupe: Editions Jasor, 1992.

Perret, Delphine, and Marie-Denise Shelton. Introduction to Maryse Condé special issue. *Callaloo* 18, no.3 (summer 1995): 535–37.

Perrier, Jean-Claude. "Maryse Condé: Saga en bambou." *Le Quotidien de Paris*, no.1422 (20 June 1984): 20.

———. "*Moi, Tituba, sorcière noire de Salem*." *La vie française*, 9 March 1987, 91.

Peterson, V. R. "Maryse Condé: Unravelling the Unexplored." *Essence*, February 1993, 52.

Pied, Henri. "'Césaire méritait le Nobel.'" *Antilla*, no.215 (5 November 1986): 17

Plougastel, Yann. "Maryse Condé, l'exubérante." *L'Evénement du Jeudi*, no.461 (2 September 1993): 60.

Polk, James. "Island of doubt – Maryse Condé's Tale of Death and Mys-

160

tery in Guadeloupe." *Chicago Tribune*, 23 April 1993, 6 (Tribune books section).

"Portrait de femme: Maryse Condé. . . ." *TV Magazine/France-Antilles*, no.121 (1992): 6–8.

Proulx, Patrice June. "Speaking from the Margins: Exiles, Madwomen and Witches in Marie Cardinal, Maryse Condé and Myriam Warner-Vieyra." Ph.D. diss., Cornell University, 1991.

R., S. de la *Traversée de la Mangrove*." *Le Quotidien de Paris*, 7 February 1990, 11.

Rabathaly, Rudy. "Maryse Condé: 'Rechercher la diversité des voix.'" *France-Antilles Magazine*, 11 September 1993, 44–45.

Radiguet, Chloé. "*Traversée de la Mangrove*." *Bonne Soirée*, 14 March 1990, 6.

Rakotoson, Michèle. "Maryse Condé, *Moi, Tituba, sorcière noire de Salem*." *Equateur*, no.2 (January–February 1987): 88.

Rambo, Betty. "Maryse Condé: Une noire de Salem." *Beauté Black Magazine*, January–February 1987, 125.

——. "Rentrée littéraire du côté des femmes. . . ." *Américas*, February 1988, 38.

Ramos Isern, Magda. "Enmarañado país." Translation of *Pays mêlé* as master's thesis, University of Puerto Rico, 1988.

Rea, Annabelle M. "Condé, Maryse: *Pays mêlé*." *French Review* 60, no.6 (May 1987): 905–6.

Réka, Lili. "Maryse Condé: Où sont mes racines?" *Marie-Claire*, December 1985, 96–97.

Riembault, Fabienne. "*Les derniers rois mages*." *Notes Bibliographiques*, June 1992, 793.

Rihoit, Catherine. "L'expérience des limites." *Marie-Claire*, June 1992, 274.

Rosello, Mireille. "Caribbean Insularization of Identities in Maryse Condé's Work: From *En attendant le bonheur* to *Les derniers rois mages*." *Callaloo* 18, no.3 (summer 1995): 565–78.

——. *Littérature et identité créole aux Antilles*. Paris: Karthala, 1992.

——. "One More Sea to Cross: Exile and Intertextuality in Aimé Césaire's *Cahier d'un retour au pays natal*," trans. Robert Postawsko. *Yale French Studies* 2, no.83 (1993): 176–95.

Rosset, Pierrette. "L'Héritier – *Les derniers rois mages*." *Elle*, 4 May 1992, 84.

——. "Maryse Condé – Une histoire de famille." *Elle*, 21 December 1987, 59.

——. "Maryse Condé: Retour à la Guadeloupe." *Elle*, 20 October 1986, 71.

Rouch, Alain, and Gérard Clavreuil. *Littératures nationales d'écriture française*. Paris: Bordas, 1987.

Roy, Édouard. "*Traversée de la Mangrove*." *La Voix du Combattant*, March 1990, 36. .

Rushing, Andrea Benton. "An Annotated Bibliography of Images of Black Women in Black Literature." *CLA Journal* 21, no.3 (March 1978): 435–42.

——. "An Annotated Bibliography of Images of Black Women in Black Literature." *CLA Journal* 25, no.2 (December 1981): 234–62.

S., D. "*Traversée de la Mangrove*." *Lire*, March 1990, 51.

Sainville, Léonard. "*Dieu nous l'a donné* de Maryse Condé." *Présence Africaine*, no.84 (4th quarter 1972): 136–38.

Savigneau, Josyane. "Ce que les Français ont lu cette année." *Le Monde*, 10 July 1987, 11.

——. "Maryse Condé et la sorcière noire." *Le Monde*, 19 December 1986, 17.

Scarboro, Ann Armstrong. Afterword to Maryse Condé, *I, Tituba, Black Witch of Salem*, trans. Richard Philcox. Charlottesville: University Press of Virginia, 1992.

——. "Womb of Shadow – *Moi, Tituba, sorcière, Noire de Salem*." *American Book Review*, January–February 1988, 8.

Schwarz-Bart, Simone. *Hommage à la femme noire*. Paris: Editions Consulaires, 1989.

Seaman, Donna. "Condé, Maryse. *Tree of Life*." *Booklist* 89, no.1 (1 September 1992): 31.

"*Segu* by Maryse Condé." *Washington Post Book World*, 19 June 1988, 12.

Sellin, Eric. "*Dieu nous l'a donné. . . .*" *Books Abroad* 47, no.3 (summer 1973): 601.

Séphocle, Marie-Line. "La réception de Maryse Condé et Simone Schwarz-Bart en Allemagne." In Maryse Condé, Delphine Perret, Michael Lucey, and Ann Smock, eds., *L'Héritage de Caliban*. Guadeloupe: Editions Jasor, 1992.

Serbin, Sylvia. "Le dernier roi mage." *Brune*, no.5 (June–August 1992): 11.

Servet, Michel. "Maryse Condé: Fini la France, fini l'Afrique, je rentre chez moi." *Jeune Afrique Magazine*, November 1985, 26–27.

Sévry, Jean. "Discussion après l'intervention de A. M. Jeay et table ronde de conclusion." *Nouvelles du Sud*, May–July 1986, 138–41.

Shelton, Marie-Denise. "Condé: The Politics of Gender and Identity." *World Literature Today* 67, no.4 (autumn 1993): 717–22.

——. "Condé, Maryse. *Moi, Tituba, sorcière . . . noire de Salem.*" *French Review* 61, no.2, December 1987, 314–15.

——. "Literature Extracted: A Poetic of Daily Life." *Callaloo* 15, no.1 (winter 1992): 167–78.

——. "Women Writers of the French-Speaking Caribbean: An Overview." In Selwyn R. Cudjoe, ed., *Caribbean Women Writers*. Wellesley MA: Calaloux Publications, 1990.

Shungu, Ekanga. "La Bibliothèque de . . . Maryse Condé." *Jeune Afrique*, no.1216 (April 1984): 66–67.

——. "*Ségou.*" *Jeune Afrique Magazine*, May 1984, 74.

Silenieks, Juris. "Maryse Condé: *Ségou: Les murailles de terre.*" *World Literature Today* 59, no.2 (spring 1985): 309–10.

Simson, Maria. "*Crossing the Mangrove* by Maryse Condé, translated by Richard Philcox." *Publishers Weekly* 242, no.4 (23 January 1995): 65.

Slavin, J. P. "In Deep Voodoo." *Washington Post Book World*, 26 February 1995, 5.

Smith, Arlette. "Conversation with Condé: A Review of Françoise Pfaff's *Entretiens avec Maryse Condé.*" *Callaloo* 18, no.3 (summer 1995): 707–9.

——. "*Entretiens avec Maryse Condé* by Françoise Pfaff." *CLA Journal* 37, no.4 (June 1994): 467–72.

——. "Maryse Condé's *Hérémakhonon*: A Triangular Structure of Alienation." *CLA Journal* 32, no.1 (September 1988): 45–54.

——. "Sémiologie de l'exil dans les oeuvres romanesques de Maryse Condé." *French Review* 62, no.1 (October 1988): 50–58.

——. "The Semiotics of Exile in Maryse Condé's Fictional Works." *Callaloo* 14, no.2 (spring 1991): 381–88.

Smith, Michelle. "Reading in Circles: Sexuality and/as History in *I, Tituba, Black Witch of Salem.*" *Callaloo* 18, no.3 (summer 1995): 602–7.

Smith, Valerie. "Island Requiem Sings of Colonial Past." *Emerge* 6, no.6 (April 1995): 57.

Smock, Ann. "Maryse Condé's *Les derniers rois mages.*" *Callaloo* 18, no.3 (summer 1995): 668–80.

Snapp, Joanne. "Condé, Maryse. *I, Tituba, Black Witch of Salem.*" *Library Journal* 117, no.12 (July 1992): 120.

——. "*Tree of Life*: A Novel of the Caribbean." *Library Journal* 117, no.14 (September 1992): 212.

Snitgen, Jeanne. "History, Identity and the Constitution of the Female Subject: Maryse Condé's *Tituba.*" *Matatu: Journal of African Culture and Society* 3, no.6 (1989): 55–73.

Soestwohner, Bettina Anna. "Narrative Margins in Maryse Condé's Novels *Hérémakhonon* and *La vie scélérate*: Between the Myth of History and the Memories of the Mothers." Ph.D. diss., University of California, Irvine, 1994.

——. "Uprooting Antillean Identity: Maryse Condé's *La colonie du nouveau monde.*" *Callaloo* 18, no.3 (summer 1995): 690–706.

Sourieau, Marie-Agnès. "*Traversée de la Mangrove*: Un champ de pulsions communes." *Francofonia*, no.24 (spring 1993): 109–22.

——. "*La vie scélérate* de Maryse Condé – Métissage narratif et héritage métis." In Maryse Condé and Madeleine Cottenet-Hage, eds., *Penser la créolité*. Paris: Karthala, 1995.

Spear, Thomas C. "Individual Quests and Collective History." *World Literature Today* 67, no.4 (autumn 1993): 723–30.

——. "Jouissances carnavalesques: Représentations de la sexualité." In Maryse Condé and Madeleine Cottenet-Hage, eds., *Penser la créolité*. Paris: Karthala, 1995.

Spire, Arnaud. "Tous des sorcières." *L'Humanité*, 30 October 1986, 22.

Steinberg, Sybil. "*I, Tituba, Black Witch of Salem.*" *Publishers Weekly* 239, no.31 (13 July 1992): 45.

——. "*Segu.*" *Publishers Weekly* 231, no.4 (6 February 1987): 84.

Taleb-Khyar, Mohamed B. "An Interview with Maryse Condé and Rita Dove." *Callaloo* 14, no.2 (spring 1991): 347–66.

Tamba, Coura. "Le retour aux sources." *Elite Madame*, no.13 (June–July 1990): 13.

Thierry, R. "Le dernier roman de Maryse Condé: *Moi, Tituba, sorcière noire de Salem.*" *Confidences*, November 1986, 41–42.

Thornton, Lawrence. "The Healer." *New York Times Book Review*, 16 July 1995, 17.

"*Tree of Life.*" *Chicago Tribune*, 21 November 1993, 8 (Tribune books section).

"*Tree of Life.*" *Publishers Weekly* 239, no.29 (29 June 1992): 50–51.

Tucker, Neely. "America the Vast and Cruel." *Detroit Free Press*, 4 October 1992, 7G.

V., L. "La *Traversée de la Mangrove*." *Témoignages*, 28 June 1990, 18.

Van Hove, Julie. "Des auteurs qui 'brodent françé comme pas un.'" *Pages*, December 1987, 13.

Vanoyeke, Violaine. "Maryse Condé: Conte sensuel." *Le Quotidien de Paris*, 8 April 1992, 26.

Wallace, Karen Smyley. "Women and Identity: A Black Francophone Female Perspective." *Sage* 2, no.1 (spring 1985): 19–23.

Wauthier, Claude. "Maryse Condé: *Moi, Tituba, sorcière noire de Salem*." *La Quinzaine littéraire*, 16 February 1987, 8.

——. "Pèlerinage aux sources dans une famille bambara." *La Quinzaine littéraire*, no.421 (16–31 July 1984): 14.

Wennefer, Tehuti. "Characters in a Mirror." *West Africa*, 29 July 1985, 1548.

White, Sarah. "Scarred by history." *Women's Review of Books* 12, no.10–11 (July 1995): 42–43.

Williams, John. "*La parole des femmes – Essais sur des romancières des Antilles de langue française*." *Black Scholar* 17, no.4 (July–August 1986): 57.

Wilson, Elizabeth. "Le voyage et l'espace clos – Island and Journey as Metaphor: Aspects of Women's Experience in the Works of Francophone Caribbean Women Novelists." In Carole Boyce Davies and Elaine Savory Fido, eds., *Out of the Kumbla: Caribbean Women and Literature*. Trenton NJ: Africa World Press, 1990.

Wood, Jacqueline E. "Cracked Roots: Identity in Maryse Condé's *Heremakhonon*." Master's thesis, Florida Atlantic University, 1991.

Wylie, Hal. "The Cosmopolitan Condé, or Unscrambling the Worlds." *World Literature Today* 67, no.4 (autumn 1993): 763–68.

——. "Guadeloupe . . . *La colonie du nouveau monde* by Maryse Condé." *World Literature Today* 68, no.3 (summer 1994): 619–20.

——. "*Heremakhonon*." *World Literature Today* 57, no.1 (winter 1983): 157.

——. *"Pays mêlé* suivi de *Mama Ya."* World Literature Today 60, no.4 (autumn 1986): 679.

Xenakis, Françoise. "Honni soit qui Mali pense!" *Le Matin,* 22 May 1984, 19.

Yoder, Hilda van Neck. *"Tim tim! Bois sec!. . . ."* World Literature Today 56, no.1 (winter 1982): 163–64.

Zimra, Clarisse. "Condé, Maryse. *Une saison à Rihata."* French Review 56, no.1 (October 1982): 165–66.

——. "Condé, Maryse. *Ségou – Les murailles de terre."* French Review 59, no.3 (February 1986): 484–85.

——. "Righting the Calabash: Writing History in the Female Francophone Narrative." In Carole Boyce Davies and Elaine Savory Fido, eds., *Out of the Kumbla: Caribbean Women and Literature.* Trenton NJ: Africa World Press, 1990.

Zirilli, Anne. "Au nom de la vie." *Femina,* February 1987, 42.

Index

About the Author

Of Alsatian and Guadeloupean origins, Françoise Pfaff was born, raised, and educated in Paris. She has resided for the past twenty years in the United States, where she is a professor of French at Howard University in Washington DC. She has published widely on African and Caribbean literatures and cinemas. She is author of *The Cinema of Ousmane Sembene, A Pioneer of African Film* (1984) and *Twenty-five Black African Filmmakers* (1988), both from Greenwood Press (Westport, Connecticut), and *Entretiens avec Maryse Condé* (1993), Editions Karthala (Paris). (Photo by María Roof.)